Between us there is but a narrow wall,
and by sheer chance; for it would take
merely a call from your lips or from mine
to break it down,
and that without a sound.

The wall is builded of your images.
R. M. Rilke, The Book of Hours

Following this tradition...the world is represented as if its
beings all contained their own source of light. Light is imma-
nent in this world of medieval things, and they reach the eye of
the beholder as sources of their own luminosity.
Ivan Illich, In the Vineyard of the Text

Christ is the icon of the invisible God
and the firstborn of all creation.
Colossians 1:15

Table of Contents

Introduction

The Spiritual Ethos of the Christian East

The churches of the Christian East in their doctrine, liturgies and traditional customs, have a vibrant sense of the central mysteries of the Christian faith.[1] They believe in God as a Trinity of Persons revealed to us in the incarnate Son and Word, Jesus Christ, and most especially in his holy and glorious *Pascha,* the mystery of his redeeming death and resurrection. Through it, the eternal *koinonia,* or community of the Trinity, reveals itself in order to draw us into relationship with God and one another. Eastern Christians pray and worship in the power of the Holy Spirit, who proceeds eternally from the Father, rests upon the Son, and is sent into the world to make God's people holy. They have a deep sense of both the transcendence of God who is absolutely other, and yet of his close relationship with

1 In this book 'the Christian East' refers to the Orthodox, Oriental Orthodox and Eastern Catholic churches. Detailed scholarly information on the history and cultural traditions of Eastern Christianity can be found in *The Oxford Dictionary of Byzantium,* (New York/Oxford, 1991), ed. by A. Kazhdan. *The Blackwell Dictionary of Eastern Christianity,* (Oxford, 1999), ed. by K. Parry, D. J. Melling, D. Brady, S. H. Griffith and J. F. Healy, is also full of useful information in a more accessible form. On Byzantine Orthodoxy, see J. Pelikan, *The Spirit of Eastern Christendom 600-1700* (Chicago, 1974). Two older books remain outstanding introductions to Orthodox theology and life: V. Lossky, *The Mystical Theology of the Eastern Church* (London, 1957) and S. Bulgakov, *The Orthodox Church* (London 1935). For a good general presentation of Orthodoxy up to the present day, K. Ware's, *The Orthodox Church* (London, 1993) is still indispensable. Two large books by M. Zibawi, both with fine illustrations, *The Icon, its Meaning and History* (Collegeville, 1993) and *Eastern Christian Worlds* (Collegeville, 1995) give a valuable visual impression of both the Orthodox and Oriental Orthodox traditions. However, to really experience the ethos of Eastern Christianity one should attend a celebration of the divine liturgy in an Eastern church.

creation, since the latter is itself the manifestation in time of God's eternally vibrant, creative inner world.

Eastern Christians love to celebrate solemn liturgical worship in the divine liturgy (the eucharist), and in the feasts and offices of the liturgical year. They love also the beauty of their church building as a microcosm of the universe, the place where God's glory appears. Yet much as they delight in communal worship, they also display a strongly monastic ethos, which insists on the need for perpetual prayer of the heart centred on the name of Jesus, the sacrament of his presence. To facilitate the concentration required by such prayer, they have developed a profound ascetical system for training the body and the mind, to make them more attentive to the presence of God. The immediate aim of such asceticism is the cultivation of *hesychia*, a complete stilling of the outer and inner senses resulting in a state of concentration, receptive to the light of grace.

They believe that this grace of God is poured out on us in his divine energies, the transfiguring *Thaboric* light which is the Holy Trinity manifesting itself to us, and that the uncreated light is concentrated in the body of Christ which we receive in the eucharist. Hence the goal of the Christian life is *theosis,* or deification. This means sharing in God's own qualities and attributes – above all in his boundless, incorruptible life – by communion with the transfigured body of Christ in the power of the Holy Spirit.

Eastern Christians love and venerate Mary as the *Theotokos*, or God-bearer, and the saints as *Pneumatophoroi*, or Spirit-bearers, who witness to the truth of Christ through martyrdom and charity. They insist that *plerophoria*, or conscious awareness of the Holy Spirit, who dwells in the heart, granting it the joy of inner freedom, is the normal fruit of baptism. They profess their belief in the goodness of the body, destined as it is to rise again with Christ, who will transform it into the likeness of his own glorious body (Philippians 3:21) when he returns in the *Parousia*, the glory of his second coming.

These truths, so strongly manifest in Eastern Christianity, are common to all Christians but they have given rise in the East to a particular ethos of life and worship, a contemplative, mystical vision of Christianity, in which transfiguration by the Holy Spirit is strongly emphasised.[2]

Of course the history of the Eastern churches indicates that they have not always lived their tradition in its fullness. Yet without romanticising it or devaluing the spiritual depths in Western Christianity, it is true that this contemplative ethos is often lived among them with an intensity and authenticity reminiscent of the first centuries of Christian history.[3] I have experienced the truth of this myself, not only in Greece, but in India and in the *Diaspora*, the communities of Eastern Christians in Western Europe and the United States of America. My aim in writing this book is to spread the knowledge of this contemplative ethos by means of meditations on the Glenstal icons, so as to help those who wish to pray and meditate on the mysteries of Christ, in the spirit of the Christian east.

2 Eastern Christianity is not limited to Orthodoxy alone: the Oriental Orthodox and Eastern Catholic traditions also need to be considered. For reliable information on the history and life of the ancient Church of the East and the Oriental Orthodox churches see *A History of Eastern Christianity* (London 1967), by A.S. Atiya, and *Light From the East* (Toronto, 1988), ed. by H. Hill. On the Eastern Catholic Churches see *Rome and the Eastern Churches* (Edinburgh, 1992), by A. Nichols OP.

3 Eastern Christianity generally retains a vivid sense of continuity with the primitive church.

The Role of the Icon in the Church

The icon is a kind of a synthesis of the spiritual truths and values of Eastern Christianity.[4] It is much more than just a religious painting, or a didactic aid. It is a sacramental medium, a meeting point between the divine uncreated light and the human heart. Its visible, created beauty is a luminous epiphany, a 'place' of manifestation, where prayer gains access to the uncreated beauty of God's grace and truth.[5]

The subjects depicted in the icons reveal the principal mysteries of Christ: his incarnation, death, resurrection and ascension, and the sending of the Holy Spirit at Pentecost. But they also show the saints, and in particular Mary the *Theotokos*, or God-bearer, whose faces shine with the

4 In locating the icon within the general history of Byzantine art, four recent introductions to Byzantine art are indispensable. See *Early Christian and Byzantine Art* (London/New York, 1997) by John Lowden, *Byzantine Art and Architecture, An Introduction* (Cambridge, 1993) by Lyn Rodley, *The Art of Byzantium* (London, 1998 by Thomas Mathews and *Byzantine Art* (Oxford, 2000) by Robin Cormack. On the rise and development of the icon, see *The Icon, Holy Images* (London, 1978) by K. Weitzmann and *The Icon* (London, 1982) by the same author with contributions by others. An excellent introduction to all aspects of the earlier Russian tradition can be found in *The Art of Holy Russia, Icons from Moscow, 1400-1600* (London, 1998).

5 For a theological introduction to iconographic theory, see *The Theology of the Icon* (New York, 1978) by L. Ouspensky and *The Meaning of Icons* (New York, 1982) by L. Ouspensky and V. Lossky. P. Evdokimov's *The Art of the Icon, A Theology of Beauty* (California, 1990) trans. by S. Bigham is often inspiring, but needs to be read critically. It suggests a hint of 'cultural imperialism' which risks denigrating the spiritual values found in non-iconic art. Two accessible popular accounts are *Doors of Perception – Icons and their Spiritual Significance* (Oxford, 1987) and *Festival Icons for the Christian Year* (Oxford, 2000) both by John Baggley. In general too much should not be made of the anonymity of the artists. Robin Cormack's work, referred to above, on post-Byzantine art, argues persuasively that in the Greek world iconographers were established (and recorded) figures in their communities.

transfiguring light of grace, communicated to them by the Spirit and manifested in them through contemplative prayer.

The mysteries of Christ that we celebrate in liturgical worship are not just historical events or objectively revealed truths, but spiritual realities, through which the transcendent Trinity has revealed itself in space and time. Thanks to the ascension of Christ and the descent of the Holy Spirit of Pentecost, they have become for us an unfailing spring of grace. Baptised into Christ's death and resurrection, the Spirit continuously opens them to us for our participation every time we celebrate the liturgy. He infuses their energy into our hearts as we pray and worship.

The icons allow this action of the Holy Spirit in liturgical worship to extend beyond the celebration into personal prayer, for the same mysteries we encounter in the liturgy are vividly represented in them. Contemplated in the icons, the mysteries of Christ make a powerful impression on the heart, filling it with grace and giving it a mystical communion with the Holy Trinity and the invisible world of angels and saints. Icons keep the central mysteries of the faith constantly before us, reminding us of what is most essential in the Christian revelation. They foster a sense of the *perichoresis*, or mutual interpenetration, that should exist between theology and prayer as they weave through one another in worship.[6]

6   Among the earliest monastic authorities, Evagrius (c. 345 – 399) affirmed the indivisible unity of theology and prayer. See *Evagrius Ponticus, The Praktikos and Chapters on Prayer*, (Kalamazoo / Michigan, 1981), trans. J. E. Bamberger. Much of the theological renaissance in twentieth century Roman Catholicism was inspired by a similar desire to reconcile the two after centuries of compartmentalisation. Within the last hundred years modern Orthodox theology has begun to escape from the theological rationalism in which it was trapped from the sixteenth

The Glenstal icons, coming as they do from the Christian East, embody this mystical ethos of prayer, worship and living theology. They represent the presence of the East within the West, of Orthodoxy in a Roman Catholic monastery.

The Icons and *Lectio Divina*:
Ancient and Post-Modern Insights

This book provides an opportunity to contemplate the icons, to meditate on the mysteries they depict and to pray with them. Its shape reflects the ancient, hallowed monastic custom of *lectio divina*, or sacred reading, which has undergone something of a renaissance in recent years, not only in monasteries but among many lay people as well.[7] This is one of the spiritual treasures of Western Christianity and especially of the Benedictine and Cistercian traditions.

Lectio divina is a spiritual method developed in early and medieval monasticism for focusing the mind in prayer, and uniting the whole of one's life in contemplative attention to the word of God in holy scripture. Traditionally it involves three components:

The first is an attentive reading of a text such as a section of the scriptures, a piece of the liturgy or a poem. This is the *lectio* itself. A short piece of scripture is read aloud and 'bitten off' as food for the soul.

century onwards. See *Being as Communion: Studies in Personhood and the Church* (New York, 1985) by John Zizioulas, for a theological vision based on authentic patristic and liturgical categories of thought, located within a perspective derived from modern personalist philosophies.

7   Numerous Benedictine monasteries can testify to the interest shown in *lectio divina* today, both among monastics and lay people. See *Sacred Reading* (Missouri, 1996) by M. Casey OCSO for the mechanics of *lectio*. Much insight is also contained in *In the Vineyard of the Text* (Chicago, 1993) by Ivan Illich.

Reading leads to the second stage: *meditatio*. This entails a slow rumination of the text, 'chewing it over' in the mouth and mind until its message is implanted in the heart. This is the oldest meaning of *meditatio*. It is not primarily an intellectual exercise but an activity of learning by heart.

Such rumination in turn leads to the third stage, *oratio*, or prayer. Spontaneous acts of adoration and supplication leap like sparks from the iron of the heart as the word of God strikes upon it. The whole process is a strenuous one, an activity involving eyes, ears, mouth and mind.

Lectio divina has a particular advantage as a method of prayer in that the text itself provides both a launching pad for ascent to God, and a secure base on which to rest when the wings of faith and prayer grow tired. When dryness or boredom intervene and acts of prayer refuse to flow, then the one who prays simply returns to the text, which thus becomes a kind of spiritual support system. Prayer is sustained and supported by the word of God. There is no need when praying, to hang, aching and empty, in a spiritual vacuum. At times of difficulty, one simply goes back to the text or moves on to another one.[8] It is a kind of journey in the spiritual life. As the early monks believed, the main aim

8 Boredom, dryness and routine may appear in the life of prayer as in every other area of human experience. Significant thinkers in the Roman Catholic tradition (especially among the medieval Dominicans and early-modern Carmelites) have stressed that long periods of ennui can be valuable in weaning one away from superficial consolations. By conferring a mystical share in Christ's sufferings they may even have a redemptive value. In general, with a few notable exceptions, such as the Russian St Tikhon of Zadonsk (1727-1783), this kind of experience is not common in the East, where more emphasis is placed on the state of joy that characterises deep prayer. Careful discernment is necessary to distinguish spiritually valuable dryness as a grace of prayer, from ordinary tiredness or lack of energy.

of *lectio divina* is not just to acquire information about religious topics, but to linger for long periods in the presence of God so as to become receptive to his light.

However, modern culture in many parts of the world is increasingly visual, with images tending to dominate our thinking more and more. Indeed in post-modern thought the very notion of a 'text' itself has greatly expanded beyond written words.[9] Everything that presents itself to us for our consideration is a kind of 'text.' It assumes a network or web of relationships since every text inhabits an inter-textual world, which comes to be within a wider context of social and linguistic interaction. No human being, however isolated she may choose to become, can exist outside such social contexts. They are simply unavoidable since they are built into the structure of human existence

The liturgical tradition of the churches and the icons of the Christian East, with their symbolic language based on images, can speak powerfully to this modern situation. Hence the 'texts' presented in this book are not principally written words: they are in fact the icons themselves, since in the traditional language of Orthodoxy icons are actually

---

9 For a good short introduction to post-modernity in general and post-modernist theological method in particular, see G. Ward, 'Postmodernism' in *The Oxford Companion to Christian Thought* (ed. by A. Hastings, A. Mason and H. Pyper, Oxford, 2000). Ward's more convoluted treatment in *The Modern Theologians* (ed. by D. F. Ford, Oxford, 1999), pp. 585-601, like quite a lot of post-modernist exposition, at times risks a descent into jargon. This should not be allowed to obscure the important truths within the post-modern project nor the value of them for Christian theology and spirituality. In *Theological Hermeneutics: Development and Significance* (London, 1991), W. G. Jeanrond gives a comprehensive overview of the whole subject, along with a critical but sympathetic account of Derrida's work. He observes that full adherence to Derrida's positions would effectively cancel any possibility of meaning in theology.

written rather than painted.[10] They have long been understood in the Christian East as a visual manifestation of the word of God, or as a symbolic actualisation of the gospel.

Therefore, in adopting the traditional method of *lectio divina* for praying with the icons, 'reading' refers to a contemplative engagement with the icon itself as the primary text. This reading process is every bit as strenuous and engaged as conventional reading in the monastic sense. Instead of literally mulling over written texts in the traditional way, one 'reads' the imagery of the icon, wrestling with its 'grammar' and iconographic signs, in an attempt to learn and speak the language of the Christian mysteries and of prayer.

Orthodox theology, taking its inspiration from the New Testament, recognises that in Jesus, the incarnate Word of God, the dichotomy of seeing and hearing has been removed. We 'see' the Word through the medium of the flesh of Christ and its extension in the icon.[11] The essential texts here are the icons themselves.

Meditatio in this sense then, means developing a visual receptivity which allows the imagery of the icons to enter deeply into the soul so as to awaken a spiritual response to the mysteries they mediate. In this contemplative process, connections are opened up and consciousness is widened. The world of relationships inhabited by the icons, that is, their inter-textuality, becomes apparent. This inter-textuality locates them within three wider fields, each of which is, in different ways, a social context .

10 The notion of reading an icon is therefore a highly traditional one.
11 See 1 John 1: 1-3, and the remarks by Hans Urs von Balthasar in *The Glory of the Lord: A Theological Aesthetics*, 1. *Seeing the Form* (Edinburgh, 1982), trans. by E. Leiva-Merikakis, J. Fession and J. Riches, pp. 232-241.

The most basic context is that of the historical-cultural settings of late antiquity and the medieval world – Byzantium, Russia, Eastern Europe and the Middle East – the social matrices in which a distinctively iconographic art emerged. To divorce the icon from this context is to tear it from its historical roots and cultural origins since the Christian faith, and the icon itself, emerged in history.[12] The ethos of Eastern Christianity has been definitively shaped by its local, ethnic, historically rooted character. Abstracting the icon from this context in the interests of some eternally valid 'sacred art' entails a betrayal of its origins and a denial of the incarnate reality it seeks to affirm.

The second context is that of the liturgical life and traditional practices of the Eastern churches. Icons belong to the world of worship typical of the developed Byzantine

12 Much recent Byzantine art history is revisionist, critical of interpretations of the icon using the familiar categories of Western art historians. Byzantinists aim to locate icons more fully in the social, political and ecclesial contexts in which they were produced. Semiotics has proved a useful hermeneutical tool in this field. See *Writing in Gold – Byzantine Society and Its Icons* (London, 1985) and *Painting the Soul – Icons, Death Masks and Shrouds* (London, 1997), both by R. Cormack. For a particularly incisive account of the rise and function of icons in Byzantine society, see Averil Cameron's 'The Language of Images' in 'Studies in Church History', vol. 28, *The Church and the Arts* (ed. by D. Wood, Oxford, 1995.). Such revisionism with its strong sense of context is a useful corrective to the reading of iconography through the lens of twentieth-century Russian religious philosophy, an approach typifying most popular books on the icon. The revisionists teach us to look at Crusader, post-Byzantine and Venetian icons not as decadent works of art, but as deserving of interest in their own right. They set them firmly in their social context and emphasise the crucial role of the patron. This does not make them any less spiritual, but overcomes the false assumption that they simply emerge from prayer. For a brilliant, if somewhat tendentious statement of the traditional (largely Russian) theology of icons, see the book by the priest, polymath and martyr Pavel Florensky, *Iconostasis* (New York, 1986), trans. by D. Sheehan and O. Andrejev.

church building, and the complex system of liturgical rites celebrated within it.[13] Orthodox theologians like to observe that the church building itself is a kind of icon, manifesting the structure of the cosmos, with the nave symbolising earth, the altar area heaven, and the dome the highest heavens. The church building is thus a complex semiotic structure. It provides a setting for the liturgy, in which all aspects of the cosmos in their inter-relationship are represented. Icons are most at home in this ritual system. To divorce them from their architectural and ritual context is to forget that they are primarily functional objects, operating within a total 'language' of sacred signs. They are part of a ritual structure, the liturgy, expressing the religious life of real communities.

The third context is the opening that the icon makes beyond itself, not simply temporally by its historical and cultural references, nor 'horizontally', in ritual and ecclesial inter-relationships, but 'vertically', through its references to God and the transcendent mysteries it mediates, by means of paint and wood. To divorce it from this context is to undermine its significance as a sacramental object leading the one who contemplates it into communion with

---

13 The standard account of the Byzantine Eucharistic liturgy in the context of its symbolic setting is that of H. J. Schulz, *The Byzantine Liturgy, Symbolic Structure and Faith Expression* (New York, 1986). Another useful study is Christopher Walter's *Art and Ritual of the Byzantine Church* (London, 1982). Robert Taft in 'Liturgy and Eucharist', in *Christian Spirituality*, *II* (ed. J. Rait, London, 1987) gives a customarily trenchant account of how divorced liturgy became from Christian life in the late Byzantine period (1204-1453), thus warning against a romanticisation of Eastern Christian history. But see also his two studies, 'Sunday in the Byzantine Rite' and 'The Spirit of Eastern Christian Worship', in *Beyond East and West, Studies in Liturgical Understanding* (Washington, 1984), pp. 31-48 and 111-126, where a profound empathy with Byzantine liturgy and piety is evident.

the divine 'social' basis of creation – the eternal community of the Holy Trinity and the church in heaven. As an extension of the incarnation, the icon mediates a personal communion with the divine. It invites transcendence, opening us up to the beyond, made manifest symbolically in our midst.[14]

This is its ultimate, most important social context: the access it gives to the other world, to the heavenly, eschatological dimension so often mentioned by Byzantine liturgical commentators as the goal of Christian life and worship.[15] This third context confers upon the icon an excess of meaning, an *anagogic*, or elevating function, enabling it to lift us up and insert us into the wider 'text' of the invisible world of Christian mysteries, in the vision of the new and heavenly Jerusalem.

Applying the method of *lectio divina* to the icons in this book means attempting to provide access in various ways to these three contexts (historical-cultural, liturgical-ecclesial and anagogic-eschatalogical) so as to awaken in the beholder a living sympathy with the contemplative ethos of the Christian East. The ultimate aim is to enkindle the flame of contemplative prayer, to allow the heart to be carried out of itself in *ekstasis*, a transcendent contact with God in his mysteries, through the sacramental power of the icons.

The *lectio* proposed by this book entails therefore a contemplative 'reading of the icon', while the *meditatio* is the active process of absorbing its imagery. These activities in

14 Christianity grounds this principle of mediation in the Triune God's self-gift to the world in creation, which is fulfilled in the incarnation, and the sacramental system flowing from Christ's death and resurrection. It is the Spirit who actualises it in ritual celebration.

15 Schulz, (op. cit., p.176).

turn give birth to *oratio*, or prayer. In the traditional practice of *lectio divina,* such prayer, when it shoots up out of the heart, does so in short, inspired phrases, redolent of scripture and the liturgy. Such darts of 'fiery prayer' are suggested here by means of the prayer texts which accompany the icons.[16]

These prayers are words that I have heard, read and repeated during many years of engagement with the Eastern Christian world, but in a catholic spirit, they include also words from the Western tradition. They are provided simply as an example coming from personal experience. Prayer, when it ignites in the heart, will of course produce words and sentiments unique to each person who prays.

Nor are images and words themselves the last word in prayer. Transcending both, according to one of the greatest Eastern Christian writers on prayer, there exists also the possibility of a silent communion with God beyond explicitly formulated prayers. This is a state beyond prayer itself, but it is a special gift of the Holy Spirit, given only to those who abandon themselves completely in pure faith to the action of God working in them.[17]

Learning the language of prayer, of relationship with God, means consciously entering into the dialogue God has with the human race through his Word and Holy Spirit. It means passing from an idea of God as an intellectual

16 For the notion of 'fiery prayer', see the illuminating comments by Columba Stewart, in *Cassian the Monk* (Oxford, 1998), p. 108.

17 St Isaac of Nineveh taught that prayer itself could be transcended in the experience of union with God. Although a bishop and hermit of the non-Chalcedonian Church of the East, Isaac became one of the greatest spiritual authorities in Byzantium and Russia, thanks to translations of his works. A sensitive study of his spirituality has been made by Hilarion Alfeyev, *The Spiritual World of Isaac the Syrian* (Kalamazoo/ Michigan, 2000).

concept, to an experience of the Trinity, whose mysterious presence is made known in the darkness of faith. Through the symbolism of the icons, access is gained to the absolute otherness of God in the silent union of mystical prayer: one goes through the sense of sight to the one who is beyond all vision. The meditative work demanded in absorbing the imagery of the icons is essential if prayer is to reach such a state beyond ideas, images and acts – beyond the work of the head. Only thus can the prayer we make with the body and the mind become a real 'heart-work', a deep, transforming union with God in love. The mystical traditions of Christianity, East and West, all teach that such prayer is the only source of inner peace and stability. It is the pearl of great price, the treasure hidden in the field, of which the gospel speaks (Matthew 13:44-46).

The Theology of the Icon

At the second Council of Nicaea in 787, following a turbulent period of *iconoclasm*, or the destruction of sacred images, the Byzantines definitively established the place of the icon in the Christian church and solemnly defined its meaning.[18] Further debate, after a resurgence of iconoclasm, was finally ended by another Council in 843, when the Empress Theodora restored the icons on the first Sunday in Lent. This victory of the *Iconophiles*, or those who venerate icons, has been celebrated ever since in the Byzantine Rite

18 In addition to the standard historical introductions to Byzantine art referred to above, see the following on Byzantine iconoclasm, *A Concise History of Byzantium* (New York, 2001) by Warren Treadgold, chs. 4 and 5, and *Iconoclasm* (Birmingham, 1977) ed. by A. J. M. Bryer and J. Herrin. Much useful material can also be found in *The Formation of Christendom* (Oxford, 1987) by J. Herrin.

on the same day, now known as the Sunday of Ortho-doxy.[19] The church decreed that icons were to be retained and venerated as sacred objects. As a result of these debates, Byzantine theologians developed a number of characteristic doctrines about the icon. They distinguished it carefully from idols, and related it to the rest of the Christian faith. In the earlier period of the debate, theologians such as St John of Damascus defended the goodness of matter by insisting that God affirmed the value of the world when his eternal Son took flesh and became human.[20]

From this perspective, the painting and veneration of icons emphasises the goodness of matter. God's grace comes to the human race through material means, in the flesh of Jesus and the sacramental mysteries established by him. As a direct consequence of the incarnation, the Old Testament prohibitions against images (Exodus 20:4-6; Wisdom 13:10-19), a prohibition also upheld in Islam, are not applicable to Christians. Since the incarnate Son of God has bridged the gulf between the infinity and invisibility of the Holy Trinity, and the finitude and material density of the created world, it is now possible to make an image of God.

In this way Byzantine theology affirmed the goodness of material reality and its inherent capacity for deification or transformation through the divine energies of grace.

19 The liturgical texts for the Sunday of Orthodoxy should be consulted. They have been expertly translated by Mother Mary and K. Ware in *The Lenten Triodion* (London, 1978).

20 On the technical theological issues involved see Pelikan, (op. cit.) ch. 5. For John of Damascus in particular, see G. Dragas, 'St. John Damascene's Teaching about the Holy Icons' in *Icons: Windows on Eternity* (Geneva, 1990), pp. 53-72.

The chief importance of the icon lies therefore in its christological significance.[21] It is not valued simply for its didactic usefulness as the Latin church in the West tends to emphasise, but for its sacramental capacity to continue and extend the contact God opened with humanity in the flesh of his incarnate Son. Nor is the icon simply an opening or door into the realm of the divine, as one sometimes reads in popular Byzantine texts.[22] The truth is much more profound, much more subtle.

Through the icons we are reminded of the meeting point established between God and humanity in Christ, as a result of which heaven and earth come together as one. Through the co-operation of divine grace and human artistic ability, the icon represents the invisible and intangible manifested in the visible and material, just as Christ brings together in his own person the two dimensions of the divine and human. The icon, like the Byzantine liturgy, is heaven on earth, the presence of the divine glory permeating the realm of the created world.[23]

The door was thus firmly closed in Byzantine Christianity against all dualistic tendencies that have typically denigrated the material world, denying its capacity to mediate God.[24] However, in response to earlier manifestations of superstition in some circles where icons were

21 See, C. Schönborn OP, 'Theological Presuppositions of the Image Controversy' in *Icons: Windows on Eternity*, pp. 86-92.

22 This metaphor runs the risk of encouraging an unduly static understanding of the icon. In addition, it can minimise the fact that the archetypes depicted are, in some mysterious way, rendered present *in* as well as *through* the representation. In other words, the essential analogy with the incarnation may be weakened.

23 For an interpretation of the union of heaven and earth in Byzantine liturgy, which adroitly avoids this danger see 'Heaven and Earth in Byzantine Liturgy', by K. Anatolios, in *Antiphon* 5, 2000, no. 3, pp. 21-27.

24 Pelikan, (op. cit.), pp. 216-227.

venerated, St John of Damascus also carried out an essential task. He clearly established the degrees of veneration of matter legitimate in Christian prayer, distinguishing carefully between a relative veneration given to saints and holy objects such as the altar and the gospel book, and the absolute adoration offered to the Holy Trinity alone.[25]

Adoration belongs to God the Father, to the eternal Word (incarnate as the Lord Jesus), and to the Holy Spirit. Although Mary the *Theotokos*, on account of her special role in the incarnation, is to be honoured with a higher degree of veneration than other creatures, this still falls short of the adoration due only to God.

Thus John held the balance between two potentially opposing truths. Against the danger of a superstitious use of icons, he insisted that it is not matter itself which receives adoration but God; but in defence of the goodness of matter as God's handiwork, he allowed creatures to receive a relative honour, dignified as they are by the grace of their creation and redemption.[26] Thus the icon was carefully distinguished from the idol. The victory of the iconophiles over the iconoclasts, and the solemn reaffirmation of the church's teaching on the capacity of matter for mediating the divine, were to have considerable consequences not only in Byzantine art and architecture, but in theology and spirituality as well.[27]

The great Constantinopolitan abbot, St Theodore of Stoudios, later discussed the crucial issue of what or who is

---

25 Dragas, (op. cit.), pp. 68-70.
26 Here as elsewhere in the tradition, Byzantine thought is able to hold a number of truths in creative balance.
27 Lowden, (op. cit) ch. 6. On Byzantine church decorative programmes, see *Byzantine Mosaic Decoration* (London, 1947) by O. Demus. After iconoclasm, sophisticated Byzantine programmes of church decoration really emerged. Monastic theology in the later Byzantine period

actually depicted in the icon of Christ.[28] Is it his divine nature? If so, the iconoclasts claimed, then his real humanity has been dissolved into his divinity as the monophysite heretics were generally supposed to have claimed. However, since the divine nature is invisible, it clearly cannot be depicted. But if the human nature of Christ alone is shown, this entails a resurgence of the Nestorian heresy, which (ostensibly) divided Christ into two persons, one human, the other divine.

Once again, the problem was solved on the basis of the church's authentic teaching about Christ. Since he has accomplished the union of divine and human natures in the one (divine) person of the Word,[29] this led to an important clarification regarding the icon. It depicts *persons,* not abstract *natures.* The icon of Christ shows neither his divine nature alone, since it cannot be depicted, nor his human nature alone, since it has no existence outside his divine person. It shows his divine person, manifested through his human nature, thanks to the incarnation. Iconographers do not deal in abstractions: they show us persons. Icons are thus a means of personal communion between the one who venerates them, and the holy persons depicted in and through them. Such a communion is made possible precisely by means of the mediating image. This understanding of the icon has been fruitfully developed by modern Orthodox theologians.[30]

placed special emphasis on the role of the body in prayer and on its capacity for transfiguration. See the study by G. I. Mantzaridis, *The Deification of Man: St. Gregory Palamas and the Orthodox Tradition* (New York, 1984).

28 For a discussion of the theological issues, see Pelikan, (op. cit.), ch. 3.

29 *St Theodore the Studite: On the Holy Icons* (New York, 1981) trans. by C. P. Roth.

30 See Zizioulas, (op. cit.) pp. 99-101.

Iconography is a contemplative art. It opens up the possibility of a Christian aesthetics, a redeemed way of seeing and depicting the world. But such an aesthetic calls for an *ascesis*, or ascetical struggle. Monastic tradition in all the Eastern churches insists that the human senses must be purified, converted from obsessive passions, which tend to fixate the heart on the surface appearance of things.[31] A new way of seeing must be cultivated, a discernment of the inner *logos* or divine word which grounds each thing and contains its real meaning.[32] These words or *logoi* are the presence of God in all things, his providential, directing actions in the world, guiding it to its final goal of union with him. They are the divine energies or rays of light pouring from Jesus Christ, the *Logos,* or Word of God and light of the world.[33]

Living the kind of spiritual life demanded to paint or contemplate the icon, means re-educating one's sense of sight. It entails purification from superficial seeing, a move away from a mode of perception that stops short of the

31 Spidlik, (op. cit.), pp. 329-331, dealing with this issue, summarises it nicely with the words, 'not the surface of things.'

32 Among the early monastic Fathers, Evagrius (c. 345-399), building on the thought of Origen (c. 185-c. 254), expounded with brilliance and subtlety the doctrine of the *logoi,* the words or reasons behind creation, which are grounded in Christ, the eternal *Logos.* For an excellent short account of Evagrian theology with translations of a key text (the *Ad Monachos*), see The *Mind's Long Journey to God,* (Collegeville, 1993) by Jeremy Driscoll OSB. For Evagrius, discerning the *logoi* was unthinkable without *praxis,* or purification from sin through bodily and interior asceticism, and *theoria,* or contemplative insight into nature, Scripture and God's will, obtained in prayer.

33 See Driscoll, (op. cit.), p. 72:
He who purifies himself will see
intelligible natures;
reasons of incorporeals,
a gentle monk will know.

hidden depth of things or which remains captivated only by their surface glitter. The icon reveals the spiritual in and through the material. It awakens the awareness that since, 'the world is charged with the grandeur of God' and, heaven and earth are filled with his glory (Isaiah 6:3), our senses must be cleansed if we are to perceive this.[34]

In addition, however, the very art of producing icons in Eastern Christianity is acknowledged to be a sacramental act in itself. It is a demanding art, uniting aesthetics with ascetical activity: hence the painter must be a practising Christian, who fasts, prays, receives communion and asks for the blessing of the church.[35] The artistic process is a liturgy, a service aimed at the glory of God. There is a

St Maximos the Confessor (580-622) developed these Evagrian ideas in an even more Christocentric way. See *Microcosm and Mediator. The Theological Anthropology of Maximus the Confessor* (Copenhagen, 1965) by L. Thunberg. His theology led eventually to the synthesis of St Gregory Palamas (d. 1359) who taught that the uncreated energies of grace common to all three divine persons – God himself turned to his creation – are the manifestation of the unknowable, transcendent essence of God. It is a theology of mystical depth, heavily dependent on prayer and contemplation.

34 The quotation is from the poem, 'God's Grandeur', by Gerard Manley Hopkins. See *The Poems of Gerard Manley Hopkins* (Oxford, 1970), ed. by W.H. Gardner and N. H. Mac Kenzie. Some remarks of the poet recorded in the critical notes, p. 263, are also interesting:
All things therefore are charged with love, are charged with God and if we know how to touch them give off sparks and take fire, yield drops and flow, ring and tell of him.
A similar intuition, with a strong emphasis on the purification of vision is also found in the sacred books of India. In the Isa Upanishad, one can read the following:
Behold the universe in the glory of God: and all that lives and moves on earth. Leaving the transient, find joy in the eternal: set not your heart on another's possessions…the face of truth remains hidden behind a circle of gold. Unveil it, O god of light, that I who love the true may see!
The quotation is from *The Upanishads*, (London, 1965), trans. J. Mascaro.

35 A useful introduction to the craft of icon painting can be found in *The Technique of Icon Painting* by G. Ramos-Poquí (London, 1990).

delicate interplay of forces at work in the writing of an icon, analogous in some ways to composing a piece of chant in a Gregorian style. In both cases, within a limited range sanctioned by tradition, creativity is channelled along definite lines. Those who write antiphons and icons are primarily servants of the church's worship. They are not simply free to engage in untrammelled self-expression. Instead, the ego of the painter or composer must be converted, consecrated to a greater purpose, to the revelation of the divine mysteries in building up the church.

The iconographer's art is thus a kind of priestly service. Eastern Christian liturgical texts lay great stress on the natural priesthood of humanity given by God in creation,[36] which although damaged by sin has been restored by the work of Christ in redemption. The exercise of this natural priesthood consists primarily in humankind's capacity to offer creation back to God, its source and goal. Through the skill of the iconographer conjoined with the work of grace, material elements are brought together to become a locus for the manifestation of God. There is a certain similarity in this between the icon and the eucharist, with due allowance for the fuller mode of presence mediated by the latter.[37]

---

36 This is a traditional theme in patristic literature. It has been expounded with new depth by the Romanian thinker Dumitru Staniloae. See *The Gift of the World* (Edinburgh, 2000), pp. 60-64, in which his ideas are summarised. Staniloae is one of the most important modern Orthodox theologians since he combines patristic thought with contemporary ideas in a liturgically orientated theology. See, *The Philocalial Vision of the World in the Theology of Dumitru Staniloae* by Maciej Bielawski OSB (Bydgoszcz, Poland, 1997).

37 During the iconoclastic disputes in Byzantium the church carefully distinguished between the two. Yet it did acknowledge that the icon illustrates the sacramental principle embodied in the incarnate Christ and in the eucharist. Both reveal the Spirit-bearing capacity of matter to mediate the divine presence.

In the celebration of the eucharist, bread and wine, gifts of the earth and products of human skill, are brought to the altar to be given back to God: in the words of the Roman liturgy, earth has given them but human hands have made them. Through prayer to the Father in the name of Jesus, the gift of the Holy Spirit is invoked to transform them into the glorified body and blood of Christ.[38] The iconographer too does something analogous. He brings to God products made from natural elements – egg, wood, and pigments – and through fasting and participation in the liturgy, disposes himself in prayer. The images he receives from the archetypal world of heavenly beauty become incarnate in matter, through the co-operation of human creativity with the divine creative act. The artist becomes a servant transforming matter and a medium for the manifestation of Christ's incarnate presence.

That presence is of course most fully manifested in the eucharist, but both the icon and the eucharist demonstrate that the visible creation is capable of mediating the invisible and uncreated. Both icon and eucharist point towards the ultimate liberation of matter from its enslavement to the laws of sin, necessity and death, and the glorious transformation awaiting it in the future kingdom of God's love (Romans 8:18-25).

---

38 Orthodox liturgical theologians like to insist that the transformation in the Eucharist comes from prayer for the descent of the Holy Spirit and is not the fruit of a quasi-magical incantation. See Zizioulas, pp. 160-161.

We can summarise the most important elements of the theology of the icon in the following propositions:

- The icon is a dynamic reminder that although creation is fallen, it remains essentially good. Christ, the original icon of the invisible God, did not hesitate to take it to himself in the mystery of the incarnation, thus manifesting its capacity to mediate the divine.

- The icon is a meeting-point and an epiphany. Through the union of grace with paint, wood and human skill, it brings together the heavenly realm of the archetypes depicted (Christ, the *Theotokos* and the saints) and the earthly realm of those who contemplate it in prayer. In this place of epiphany, God's graceful light, his gift of himself, can become manifest in prayer and contemplation.

- The icon is a sign of transfiguration. The iconographic process points to the natural priesthood of human creativity, the potential for transformation inherent in creation when it is in harmony with its Creator, and the beauty of God's image in humankind when it is restored by grace. The icon awakens the one who contemplates it in prayer to a transformed vision, a realisation that we are enfolded on all sides by a heavenly host of real presences.

Prayer before the Icons

Eastern Christian teaching on prayer

Eastern Christianity has developed a profound understanding of prayer, based on centuries of liturgical celebration and monastic striving for union with God.[39] For Eastern monasticism, the work of prayer is very simple. Supported by the intercession of the heavenly church, it is to awaken and maintain attention to the Holy Trinity, who is always present to us. By faith we understand that although we may talk about placing ourselves in the presence of God, this is in fact inaccurate. The Trinity is perpetually present to us: it is we who are absent to God. We are often spiritually anaesthetised, immersed in a sea of forgetfulness, oblivious to the light of the divine energies, despite the fact that they are continually shining upon us.

When we are awakened from this spiritual sleep we need to identify how God is present to us, and to find some way, some simple 'method' to help us maintain our awareness of him. Prayer means concentration and expansion:

39 *The Spirituality of the Christian East: A Systematic Handbook* (Kalamazoo/Michigan, 1986) by T. Spidlik SJ is an indispensable manual for eastern spirituality, equipping the reader with comprehensive bibliographies. See also *The Orthodox Way* (London, 1979) by K. Ware. For the Syrian tradition, see *The Syriac Fathers on Prayer* (Kalamazoo/Michigan, 1987) by S. Brock as well as his collection of articles, *Studies in Syriac Spirituality* (Poona, 1988). Basic texts for the Byzantine tradition can be found in the Greek *Philokalia*, a library of ascetical and mystical writings assembled by St Nikodemos the Hagiorite (1749-1809) and St Macarius of Corinth (1731-1805), published at Venice in 1782. There is a four volume English translation with scholarly introductions: *The Philokalia* (London, 1979-95) trans. by G. E. H. Palmer, P. Sherrard and K. Ware. Although an excellent resource, the translators sometimes seem to forget that the ascetical writers of the first millennium (e.g. St Maximos the Confessor) are common to both East and West.

concentrating on the presence of God, and at the same time allowing him to expand our consciousness towards infinity.[40]

How is God present to us? He is of course present as the One who upholds the world at every point by his creative word to the extent that if he withdrew his presence for even one moment, the entire creation would simply pass back into the nothingness out of which he calls it. This is his 'natural grace', the gift of his presence to creation and the source of our 'natural' desire for him.[41]

But Eastern Christian writers and mystics insist that this kind of presence is only the beginning. There is a deeper realisation of God's presence available to us. Through the coming of Christ and the Holy Spirit, God wishes to dwell within us in a new way: not in a mode of which we are largely unconscious, or as a kind of spiritual atmosphere in which we simply live and move and have our being (Acts 17:28), but as a lover and friend (Song of Solomon 5:10). God wants his presence to be consciously experienced by us. He wants, as St Maximos the Confessor once expressed it, the mystical marriage of the *Logos* with the human soul.

Through the mystery of baptism, God initiates us into this new mode of presence by granting us 'spiritual senses', an interior 'sensorium for the divine', through which we are enabled to perceive him spiritually within us and respond to him in love.[42] These inner senses, as they awaken and

---

40 See O. Clement, *The Roots of Christian Mysticism* (London, 1993) trans. T. Berkeley, for a general treatment of these themes with reference to many patristic texts.

41 This is how S. Bulgakov describes the inherent dynamism of creation, as it moves towards the vision of God. See *The Bride of the Lamb* (Michigan/Edinburgh, 2002) trans. by B. Jakim.

42 'Sensorium for the divine', comes from Hans Urs Von Balthasar, (op. cit.) pp. 365-417.

unfold, are educated by God in liturgy, prayer and suffering. They are a growing point of contact with him as he draws us out of ourselves towards an ever-deeper movement into his love. Conversion to a life of prayer entails the realisation that God is present to us in this way and that he calls us to respond to him in love. This is the first stage in living a deeper spiritual life.

The 'place' where God manifests his presence is the heart, the temple of the self. It is the location of the inner senses where the deepest roots of one's interiority lie, where the light of consciousness emerges out of the thick darkness of insensibility. Here, in this metaphysical matrix of the personality, body and soul are one in a unity greater than any dualism. Here too, the deepest unity between God and human beings is grounded. This is the temple, the meeting-point between God and human beings, into which he pours his Spirit in baptismal grace.[43]

Orthodox writers like to describe the spiritual life as the descent of the mind into the heart.[44] The thinking, logical, superficial intelligence symbolically associated with the head, and related to the 'outer' world by sense perception, must be baptised into a kind of inner death and resurrection. Vision must return from distracting dissipation to inner concentration. Just as Christ died, descended into the underworld and rose again, so we must die to the limited understanding of the mind and senses, by descending into this deep interiority through prayer. In the cavern of the heart we will meet the indwelling Christ. We will know an

43 For the symbolism of the temple, see Y. Congar, *The Mystery of the Temple* (London, 1962) trans. by R.F. Trevett.
44 Dumitru Staniloae describes the relationship between head and heart in Orthodox spirituality, including the 'passage' from one to the other in *Prayer and Holiness* (Fairacres, Oxford, 1987), pp. 8-11.

inner Easter and an interior Pentecost in the power of the Holy Spirit who is given to those who follow the descent of Christ.

The way down is full of risks for the passage to the heart is fraught with dangers and delusions.[45] False images may rise from the unconscious layers of the soul, blocking out the light of truth. The Orthodox insist that the one who begins the descent should do so in the company of an experienced spiritual guide who has traversed the hidden terrain of his or her own heart. This journey in and downwards, in imitation of the paschal journey of Christ, is the second stage in living a deeper spiritual life.

However, no less important than actually descending into the place of the heart, is devising some simple method to dwell habitually at this level of awareness after it has been found.[46] Orthodox tradition, particularly since the later Byzantine period, recommends a number of spiritual disciplines for doing so. One can, for instance, become attentive to one's breathing and by following the rhythm of the breath, of inhalation and exhalation, calm the inner self.[47] Breath is also a potent symbol for the Holy Spirit, the *Pneuma,* or breath of God which hovered over creation in the beginning (Genesis 1:2).

Another discipline involves paying attention to one's heartbeat, literally finding the physical place of the heart as the centre of one's existence. Here the heart of flesh is

---

45 It is a personal experience by grace, of Christ's passage through death and the underworld.

46 On the notion of method in prayer, see Spidlik, (op. cit. p. 318).

47 Byzantine writers seem to have envisaged breathing techniques as a preparation for prayer. Russian authorities warn against elaborate control of one's breath since it may have dangerous psychosomatic consequences. Such techniques should be carefully distinguished from the use of the Jesus Prayer itself.

identified as the symbol of the deepest centre of one's being. Awareness of one's heartbeat recalls the hidden, mystical presence of the inner Christ, 'the heart of the world', the infinite interiority at the centre of one's own interiority.[48]

The great advantage of such simple 'methods' is that, in addition to facilitating attention by calming down the surface levels of our being, they focus attention on physical processes which are for most of the time unconscious – except when illness intervenes. Consequently they can function as reminders of the hidden presence of God, which is normally veiled by spiritual unconsciousness. These methods serve to heighten awareness. Prayer means becoming aware, becoming conscious of the energies of Christ and the Holy Spirit as they pulse through the centre of the self. This self-discipline in practising a method of attention is the third stage in living a deeper spiritual life.

However, from the earliest centuries, the Byzantine monastic tradition has taught one special way to maintain this awareness of conscious union with God: the repeated use of the holy name of Jesus in prayer. In our day the Jesus Prayer has become one of the most widely used methods of prayer, not only in the Orthodox world, but in the Western churches as well. It is one of the greatest gifts that Orthodoxy can offer to the whole Christian community.

This is why we "pray without ceasing."
(1 Thessalonians 5:16)

---

48 Thomas Merton described this with great sensitivity in *The New Man* (New York, 1961). See also Hans Urs Von Balthasar, *Heart of the World* (San Francisco, 1979).

The Jesus Prayer

The practice of the Jesus Prayer entails repetition of the holy name within the framework of a traditional formula.[49] The inspiration for the prayer comes from various passages in the scriptures (Matthew 9:27; 26:63. Luke 18:13) while its form bears the imprint of Egyptian, Palestinian and Russian monasticism. Orthodoxy has inherited the Jewish belief that a name is, in a mysterious way, a sacramental bearer of a person's reality.[50] This is of course even more true when that person is Jesus the Christ, the eternal Son and Word of God, whose very name expresses the Lord's saving will for all creation (Matthew 1:21-24; Luke 1:31; 2:21). The details of the formulae in which the name is enshrined have varied somewhat in the course of time, but in contemporary usage shorter and longer forms are found. The short form is generally as follows:

> Lord Jesus Christ,
>
> Son of God,
>
> have mercy on me a sinner.

The long form includes mention of the Mother of God and the saints:

---

49 K. Ware, *The Power of the Name. The Jesus Prayer in Orthodox Spirituality* (Oxford, 1974). *The Name of Jesus* (Kalamazoo, 1978) by I. Hausherr SJ is the most important scholarly study but should be read in tandem with L. Gillet, *The Jesus Prayer* (New York, 1987). *The Way of a Pilgrim* (anonymous authorship, tr. by R. French, London, 1954) has had considerable influence in propagating the prayer but needs to be used with caution: see the wise comments of the Russian Elder Ambrose of Optino, quoted in *Russian Mystics* (Kalamazoo, 1980) by S. Bolshakoff, pp. 236-237. There is also a good article by G. Winkler, 'The Jesus Prayer as a Spiritual Path in Greek and Russian Monasticism' in *The Continuing Quest for God* (Collegeville, 1982), ed. by W. Skudlarek, pp. 100-113.

50 Bulgakov, (op. cit.) pp. 309-310.

Lord Jesus Christ

Son and Word of the living God,

by the prayers of your most pure Mother and of all your saints,

have mercy on us and save us.

The advantage of this longer form is that it recalls the central Christian doctrine of communion. Christians always pray as members of the body of Christ in union with the whole church in heaven and on earth. The shorter form encapsulates the very essence of the prayer, reducing it to its essential minimum. It is deeply trinitarian, since it calls on Jesus the incarnate Saviour as the Son of the eternal Father in the power of the Holy Spirit. Without the Spirit's help no one can confess that Jesus is Lord (1 Corinthians 12:3). It recalls the New Testament teaching that the Spirit of Christ, poured into the hearts of Christians enables them to cry out, 'Abba, Father', (Galatians 4:6-7; Romans 8:15-17). It is also a penitential prayer, a confession of weakness, sinfulness and the need for God's mercy.

In this book the formulae provided for the prayer have at times been expanded or contracted. They have been expanded by making mention of the particular mystery depicted in the icon displayed, and contracted in sometimes shortening the prayer to the name of Jesus with a special attribute attached to it, such as, 'Jesus my light!' In general, Orthodox tradition does not prescribe the use of the name of Jesus on its own, but tradition does sanction a variety of forms in saying the prayer. Above all, prayer should flow from what one really feels. Forms are to be respected but never slavishly followed: in the adventure of prayer one must go where the Holy Spirit leads.

The prayer is often said using a *komvoschoinion*, or

woollen prayer rope usually containing 100 knots, to count the invocations and assist concentration. This is fingered as the prayers are counted, and has become part of the monastic habit in the Byzantine tradition. It should not be confused, despite some similarities, with the Catholic rosary.

In addition it is usually accompanied by a series of physical gestures involving the repetition of the sign of the cross and prostrations of the body, the *proskynesis* or *metanoia*. This involves either a series of profound bows or full prostrations, touching the ground with the forehead. As well as being psychologically valuable, since bodily participation in prayer heightens the sense that the whole person prays, bowing is a useful reminder that no real division exists between 'private' and corporate prayer, since these gestures are common to both. Prayer is personal but never private – it is always within the communion of the church. Bowing also helps to inculcate the attitude of humility, repentance and adoration suggested by the second half of the prayer.

The aim of using the Jesus Prayer is to allow the name of the Lord, as a sacrament of his presence, to dwell in every area of one's being from the lips to the mind and heart. A gradual progression should take place from vocal repetition to silent communion, resulting in an increasing sense of the holy name dwelling in the interior of the heart.

While some Western Christians may find the penitential aspect of the prayer rather gloomy, the distinctively Eastern understanding of repentance may help to remove misapprehensions. Eastern Christians like to dwell on this aspect of human experience, not because of an inherent pessimism, but because they are deeply realistic about the human condition. Eastern Christianity in all its manifestations, and especially in its liturgical life, is a very joyful religion. The Eastern churches bless every aspect of human life from birth to death. They love to sing with joy on Easter night. But they also know that human beings are fallen creatures, existing in a state of fragmentation and much in need of grace if they are to transcend themselves and reach out in love to God and neighbour.[51] It is not for nothing that the words, 'Lord have mercy', are heard hundreds of times in Eastern Christian worship.

As so often in its teaching Eastern Christianity manages to hold together complementary truths, neither lapsing into a depressing, sin-obsessed Puritanism with no hint of paschal joy, nor falling for a facile optimism which ignores the harsh realities of sin and evil. The Jesus Prayer certainly does inculcate a sense of humility in the face of human weakness. But by its stress on spiritual sensation in the heart and the gift of tears, it allows a refined sensibility and religious emotion to grow, deep within the personality of the one who prays. Repentance culminates in joy – the joy of being forgiven and of receiving the grace to forgive others in turn.

The Eastern churches believe that such joy can be experienced in this life, by the spiritual senses and even by the body itself. Caught up in the daily cares of life we are often so beguiled by surface consciousness that our spiritual senses are simply dulled by sin. The consequence is a practical atheism based on forgetfulness of God. For the monastic tradition, East and West, the chief purpose of

---

51 St Symeon the New Theologian (949-1022) in particular, expressed the mixture of penitence and paschal joy so characteristic of Orthodox spirituality.

prayer is the overcoming of forgetfulness. Spiritual life is learning to remember the presence of God.[52]

Such remembrance demands a constant struggle to maintain deep, inner vigilance. It calls for a subtle spiritual discernment to assess if thoughts and inclinations arising in the heart come from God, or lead away from his presence. The aim of using the Jesus Prayer is to establish purity of heart by removing obstacles to the manifestation of grace. Then the Lord who dwells within the heart may reveal in it the presence of the Father in the joy of the Holy Spirit. The prayer reduces the fluctuating moods, volatile emotions and futile imaginings of the heart to *hesychia*, or silence in the presence of God. This silence is the receptacle for his light.

Praying the Jesus Prayer before the Icons

In Orthodox monasticism the Jesus Prayer is generally said with closed eyes.[53] However, it is also valuable to say the prayer while contemplating the icons, since they can help in concentrating the mind and clarifying the inner vision. There are certain practical things that one can do to prepare the heart for the work of prayer. Posture and position are important since we pray not only with the mind, but with the whole person, body and soul. The following procedures may be useful.

After kissing the icons and making the sign of the cross, one should begin with an invocation of the Holy Spirit asking for an open heart and the grace of attentive prayer. The

52 Cultivating the unceasing memory of God was central to the original monastic praxis in the desert. See Hausherr, *The Name of Jesus*, pp. 158-165.
53 Ware, *The Power of the Name*, p. 7.

Spirit and the indwelling Christ pray constantly in the heart of the believer so the aim of prayer is to join them in their praise of the Father. One must return to the centre of the self and descend consciously into the heart.

It is customary to light candles and burn incense before the icons. The smoke is a powerful symbol of prayer rising up to God from the fire of love burning in the heart (Psalm 141:2), while the lights are a reminder that Jesus is the true light giving light to all who come into the world (John 1:3-4). Gazing on the faces of Christ, the *Theotokos* and the saints, with the heart calmed and focused on God, one becomes ready to receive the light that radiates through them. Praying before the icons forces us to revise our predatory, grasping way of perceiving the world. We are inclined to think that we can capture it and reduce it to our own limited perspective. But faced with the disarming frontal gaze of the holy faces in the icons we are forced to concede that we are looked at long before we look. Our hunger to possess is challenged by their gentle look. The icon converts our vision to an objective world of spiritual realities. We enter the space of the holy: we do not reduce it to our own proportions.

It can be helpful to practice traditional *lectio divina* for a while, taking some short gospel passage or phrases from the psalms, and turning them over on the lips and in the heart. Attention should be focused on the eyes in the holy faces: they are like windows revealing the depths of the soul. The person depicted there looks directly at us, challenging our gaze, inviting us to respond. However, these eyes do not penetrate us harshly, or look at us judgementally. They appeal to us to turn and be converted from the inner chaos and confusion that so often clouds our vision.

There is nothing greedy or rapacious about the eyes in these faces. They look gently at us, for the saints are those who by grace and perseverance have quenched the fire of egotistical desire. They have expanded their hearts beyond possessiveness. The light shining through them is the infinite light of charity, the energy of God's grace mystically inhabiting the depths of their hearts. In the faces of the saints the human being as the restored image of God is revealed. This image was tarnished – but never destroyed – by sin. To heal it, God's true image, his only Son, the imprint of his being, descended into the world (Colossians 1:15; Hebrews 1:1-4). In prayer, the Holy Spirit shows us in the icons of the saints what this purified image conformed to the likeness of Christ can be.

With due attention to the rhythm of breathing and the beating of the heart, one should begin, slowly and quietly, to say the Jesus Prayer. Nothing should be forced. There should be no seeking of emotional experiences or stretching of the nerves. Orthodox spirituality has always insisted on *nepsis*, or spiritual sobriety, lest the grace that comes from God be confused with dark subconscious desires masquerading as his light.[54]

The aim is not experience itself (although experiences may come) but abandonment of self into the hands of God. Love for Jesus gives the invocation of his name a special quality of warmth and depth, for the lover loves to repeat the beloved's name, allowing its sweetness to linger on the lips. Without engaging in imaginative acts (which may be flights of fancy distracting us from the presence of God), the heart should be allowed to gently expand

---

54 Warnings against false mystical experience are regularly found throughout the *Philokalia*.

towards the full contours of the Christian mystery – to the Holy Spirit (the joy of God), to the fullness of Christ, (the paschal Saviour, crucified and risen) and to the Father (from whom both come forth, and back to whom they lead creation).

It should be allowed to expand as well towards the entire universe, to the community of all Christians. It should expand also to the heavenly church of Mary and the saints, who pray invisibly with the earthly community. It should reach out like the grace of God beyond the frontiers of Christianity to the entire human race, living and dead, whose salvation God desires with all his heart (1 Timothy 2:1-6). Above all, there should be prayer for those who deny God and destroy his human icons, in the spirit of Jesus who forgave those who crucified him (Luke 23:34).

There is room for more personal intercession too, for bringing the suffering and misery of others into the presence of God. One can sign them with the name of Jesus asking that the grace of the Holy Spirit, the *Paraclete* or Comforter, may touch them with his consolation. Such a vision of prayer entails lifting up all beings before the throne of God, holding them before him in love and anointing them with the Saviour's name.

In praying the name of Jesus before the icons therefore every aspect of one's person is involved:

- The eyes are filled with light from the faces of the saints who shine with the beauty of grace, impressing the image of God on the receptive mind.

- The mouth murmurs the holy name of the Saviour, speaking it repeatedly with reverence and love.

- The hands touch the woollen prayer-rope in harmony with the recitation of the name. By repeatedly making the sign of the cross one manually recalls Christ's death and resurrection.

- The heart, the deepest centre of the self, focused with intense attention on God's loving presence, experiences the joy of the risen Christ in the power of the Spirit, the fulfilment of all desire. Pierced by the love of God it confesses its weakness and calls upon him to show mercy to the whole creation.

Thus praying the prayer of Jesus, the Icon of the invisible God (Colossians 1:15), in the presence of the holy icons, leads to the transfiguration of the whole person, body, soul and spirit, by the fire of grace.[55] This transfiguration is the work of love, shaping the human heart in the likeness of the Holy Trinity.

55 The mystery of the Transfiguration has a central place in the spirituality of the Christian East, since it celebrates the transforming power that the death and resurrection of Christ and the coming of the Holy Spirit have opened up for creation. It became a touchstone of authentic Orthodox spirituality after the dispute over *hesychia* in the fourteenth century. See Pelikan (op. cit.) p.p. 254-270, and Spidlik, (op. cit.) pp. 340-342.

Six Essential Books for Further Reading

Those who wish to explore the history, art, theology and spirituality of Eastern Christianity could profitably concentrate on the following works and the bibliographies they provide:

K. Parry, D. J. Melling, D. Brady, S.H. Griffith and J. F. Healy (eds), *The Blackwell Dictionary of Eastern Christianity* (Oxford, 1999)

K. Ware, *The Orthodox Church* (London, 1993)

L. Rodley, *Byzantine Art and Architecture: An Introduction* (Cambridge, 1993)

V. Lossky, *The Mystical Theology of the Eastern Church* (London, 1957)

T. Spidlik, SJ, *The Spirituality of the Christian East: A Systematic Handbook* (Kalamazoo, 1986)

L. Gillet, *The Jesus Prayer* (New York, 1987)

Meditations on the Icons

In the following section of the book individual icons are displayed with accompanying meditations. These icons are always the primary texts. The meditations following them draw on various biblical and liturgical sources. Thus the icons become a point of departure for meditation on the mysteries of Christ. Each meditation is followed by a series of prayers, again from various sources, mostly biblical and Eastern Christian. A special place is given to the Jesus Prayer, often in an expanded form. As these texts are primarily intended to encourage prayer, there are no scholarly footnotes in this section, but only references to scripture (and occasionally other texts from the tradition).

With the exception of the hymn quoted in the meditation on the crucifixion, all translations from the Greek and Latin liturgies are my own work, but they have often been adapted to suit the demands of personal prayer in a contemporary context. Since biblical quotations are taken from the New Revised Standard Version, the Hebrew numeration of the psalms is followed. In referring to pseudonymous authors, traditional names will be used, out of respect for Eastern tradition. In other words, I will refer to 'Macarius' and 'Dionysios', rather than calling them 'Pseudo.' Their names are indeed the only 'pseudo' aspect to these great mystical theologians of the Christian East!

A Meditation on the Icon of Christ

May God be gracious to us and bless us,
and make his face to shine upon us.
(Psalm 67:1)

Deep in the human heart lies an insatiable longing to see the face of God and live. All religions testify to the intensity of this desire, but in the Judaeo-Christian tradition it finds its most poignant outpouring in the psalms, those songs of yearning for the presence of the living God. The psalmists speak often of this thirst for God's face:

'Come', my heart says, 'seek his face!' Your face, O Lord, do I seek. Do not hide your face from me. (Psalm 27:8-9)

Let the light of your face shine on us, O Lord. (Psalm 4:6)

Yet we also find the Lord warning Moses that no one can see God's face and live (Exodus 33:17-23). Is the deepest impulse of our being doomed to eternal frustration? Christians believe that God has in fact responded to our desire. In the prologue to St John's gospel we read that no one has ever seen God, but that the only Son who is close to the Father's heart has made him known (John 1:18). The eternal Word of God is already, even before his incarnation, the one who grounds creation with his presence. But when the Word became flesh he granted us, as the Roman liturgy for Christmas puts it, 'A new and shining vision of God's glory.' In the face of Jesus, God's incarnate Son and Word, we see the face of God, who is the source of all creation and its final end. The human face of Jesus opens to us the vision of the face of God. In Christ God has bridged the gap separating creation from himself. Yet he respects the infinite distance between him and us as the space across which he comes to us in Jesus.

The icon of Christ is a striking reminder that in Jesus, God really shared our human condition. He assumed our flesh with its pains and difficulties, but also with its joys. The eternal Son saved our human nature by joining it to himself as God, in the unity of his own person. He opened up for us the possibility of seeing God, by revealing his glory to the eyes of faith.

This Russian icon shows Christ as the *Pantokrator* or Ruler of all things, a traditional theme derived from Byzantine tradition. Russian religious sensibility, however, deepened the notion of Christ as the cosmic Ruler, by re-interpreting his power as the manifestation of his compassion.

Russian spirituality stresses that Christ's being is *kenotic* or self-emptying. It loves to dwell upon the fact that the Son of God divested himself of power and glory in becoming human. He veiled his divine majesty behind the form of a servant when he condescended to share our lot (Philippians 2:5-11).

His mysterious 'self-emptying', of which the early Christians so eloquently sang, is a great wonder, perhaps the greatest mystery of the Christian faith. The fact that Jesus the eternal Son of God appeared among us as the humble, suffering servant of the Lord, fulfilling the great prophecies of Isaiah (Isaiah 42:1-4; 49:1-7; 53:1-12; Matthew 12:15-21) is particularly highlighted in Eastern Christian worship. It serves to remind us that the true glory of the Messiah is not what we might naturally expect (1 Corinthians 1:18-25). It contradicts our human standards for judging success.

The glory of Jesus does not come from the power of the world, but is a reflection of another world – the realm of the Holy Trinity that he inhabits with the Father and the Holy Spirit.

In that higher world, there is no trace of selfish grasping, no desire to dominate or control others. All is light and love and life-giving generosity. In the heart of the Trinity there is an unending feast, an eternal banquet of self-sacrificial love. This reciprocal self-giving is what constitutes each of the divine persons in himself, for the Son receives his being from the Father and in turn confirms him in his own. In the incarnation, this eternal self-giving was translated into human terms. It revealed itself as infinite compassion for all creation. The heavenly gift of love that the Son offers to the Father in the Holy Spirit was made incarnate in his bloody death on the cross, but the motive was the same on earth as in heaven: love (1 Peter 1:20; Revelation 5:6).

All these powerful spiritual themes are contained within this Russian icon of Jesus. It corrects our understanding of God, too often based, as it is, on merely human concepts and ideas. There is certainly omnipotence displayed here, but it is far from being that of worldly power or force. On the contrary, it is a strangely paradoxical thing – the persuasive power of love. Love does not argue or command or force anyone to agree. Love knows only infinite patience. It simply suffers, but by suffering, it shines.

Jesus holds a book displaying a moving text from the Gospel, exposed for our meditation:

Come to me all you that are weary and are carrying heavy burdens, and I will give you rest. Take my yoke upon you and learn from me; for I am gentle and humble in heart and you will find rest for your souls. For my yoke is easy, and my burden is light. (Matthew 11:28-30)

These words of grace invite us to cast our worries on to God, confident that his power alone can hold us up (1 Peter: 5:7). It is a worthwhile exercise to connect Matthew's text to what comes before it in the same chapter of the gospel. Before uttering these words Jesus tells us in the strongest possible language that he alone has full knowledge of the Father and that he confers this on anyone he chooses (Matthew 11:25-27).

Both the written text and the icon stress the accessibility of God in Christ, his drawing near to us in mercy, and the power of his love for all creation: hence the tender compassion of this face, its luminous sensitivity and its power to fascinate those who pray in faith before it. How might we in our turn pray before this manifestation of compassion, this icon of the gentle, 'Russian Christ'?

We should contemplate it with receptive love, opening our souls to its compassionate eyes, allowing them to pierce the depths of our hearts. We should call upon the Lord for light, in the ancient words of the Jesus prayer: 'Jesus my light, Jesus my joy, Jesus my peace, have mercy on me.'

Gradually the icon will re-educate us, correcting any inclination we may have to think of God as harsh or distant (Psalm 103:8). It will call to mind his loving-kindness and infinite humility. We should ask, like the monks and mystics of the Christian East, that a ray of uncreated light – God's transfiguring grace – may shine in the darkness of our hearts. Then a spring of compassion will rise up in us to flow out to all who are in need.

We should implore the Lord Jesus in words from the Song of Songs, beloved of Christian mystics since the earliest times:

Let me see your face, let me hear your voice; for your voice is sweet and your face is lovely. (Song of Solomon 2: 14)

If we submit ourselves to the 'Russian Christ' revealed here and allow his light to enter our hearts, then we will experience the overwhelming assurance of his love. We will find our way towards that fully conscious experience, that joy in the Holy Spirit, which the Eastern spiritual tradition promises to the pure in heart.

Many who pray before this icon testify to its healing power. We should not, of course, interpret this in a naïve or simplistic way, for healing is a complex process. God in his providence may, in accordance with his will, heal bodily illnesses, but there are more fundamental, deep-seated 'diseases' within the human soul for which this icon provides the kind of spiritual therapy that is needed. Christ the healer, by the light of his grace, can reach into the deepest recesses of the heart and cure the passions of the soul that trap us in repetitive behaviour and prevent us from becoming free. Such diseases are the insecurities, complexes, lack of self-esteem and debilitating neurotic tendencies afflicting so many people nowadays.

It is worth repeating what Joa Bolendas, a modern mystic from Switzerland, wrote about this 'Russian Christ' after she had contemplated him in visionary prayer:

This icon of Christ, painted from a vision,
is most sacred – with a rare power of expression.
It is the icon of the Church for every kind of sick person!
Anyone contemplating this icon
Begins to be oriented spiritually toward Christ and his light.
Thus you receive light and spiritual strength.
What happens then is most holy.
By this experience not every sick person will be healed
but they will begin to become holy.
This icon must not be lost!
It is most sacred!

Prayers before the Icon of Christ

O Christ the true light enlightening all who come into this world! Lift up the light of your face on us, so that in it we may behold the unapproachable light. Guide our footsteps in the path of your commandments, through the prayers of your most pure Mother and of all the saints.
(Byzantine prayer from the first hour of the day, adapted.)

O loving Lord, Christ our God, we venerate your holy icon, asking forgiveness for our sins. Of your own free will you were raised upon the cross, to release from captivity those whom you created. We cry out to you in thanksgiving: 'When you came to save the world, you filled all things with joy!'
(Byzantine prayer for the first Sunday in Lent, adapted.)

O Christ our life, you were placed within the tomb. You destroyed death by your death and have become for us a spring of new life!
(Byzantine prayer for Holy and Great Friday evening, adapted.)

Lord Jesus, my light!
Lord Jesus, my joy!
Lord Jesus, my peace, have mercy on me!
Lord Jesus, compassionate Saviour, give light to my heart!
Lord Jesus, merciful one, open the springs of compassion in me!
Lord Jesus, radiance of the Father's glory, have pity on all who suffer!

Devotion to Mary the Mother of God first developed in the Christian East, before passing to the West. Mary is seen in the Eastern tradition as the perfect disciple who gave birth to the incarnate Word through her faith and obedience. At the same time, as the praying Virgin, she represents the mystery of the church, which, through the preaching of the gospel and the celebration of the sacramental mysteries, continues to bring Christ to birth in human hearts. Eastern icons of the holy Mother are traditionally ascribed to St Luke the Evangelist, who in addition to having been a doctor (Colossians 4:14) is believed to have been a painter also. Even if this is only a pious memory it does contain a deeper truth, for Luke in his gospel has left us the most moving portrait of Mary the Mother of Jesus.

A Meditation on the Icon
of the Tender Mother of God

My mother and my brothers are those
who hear the word of God and do it.
(Luke 8: 21)

There are many different ways of showing Mary the
Theotokos or God-bearer in the icons, but essentially they
involve two leading ideas: exposition and intimacy. Exposition, because Mary is the throne of God, on which Jesus,
the proof of God's love for all creation, is exposed for
adoration. Intimacy, because we glimpse in the relationship
of mother and child, the union of the eternal God-made-flesh with Mary the perfect mirror of the light. However,
these themes cannot be sharply divided and in this icon
there is a subtle interplay between them.

This kind of icon is called in the Greek Orthodox tradition, *Glykophilousa*, or 'sweetly kissing', since Mary holds
her child with tender, loving-kindness. It is also known as
the *Eleousa*, the merciful or compassionate type. The Mother
and child are identified by their inscriptions: *Iesous Christos*,
or Jesus Christ, for him and, *Meter Theou*, or Mother of
God, for her. He in his turn holds on to her, his hand
appearing round her neck. His halo of light contains the
cross that is to be his destiny, for he is the Lamb of God
predestined for sacrifice since before the foundation of the
world (1 Peter 1:18-20). His halo melts into hers, as if the
two lights, at one in the earthly mystery of mother and
child, were one also in the greater unity of the divine light
in him and its reflection in her who is full of grace. Yet he
alone bears the cross.

As he holds on to her, she in turn gazes out beyond him at the world, conscious of his destiny, pondering the prophecy of Simeon that a sword would pierce her own soul too (Luke 2:33-35). Their faces are pressed together as they will be at Calvary, when she receives his body from the cross. This mother represents, as in an archetype, all mothers who have held their sons in birth and death.

Mary's ability to speak to the universal human condition, to carry a multitude of projections, is a mark of her greatness, her accessibility, for every generation. But while there is pathos in the icon, there is little room for the sentimental. This child and his mother have a liturgy (a public work for God) to carry out. They have a sacred service, a mission to perform: the salvation and redemption of the world.

The icon is indeed an image of tenderness, but it shows a transfigured tenderness, lifted up into the realm of the divine. These two, human mother and heavenly child, are open to the will of God and to the demands their missions will make on them. This is no ordinary child, prophet, priest or king: he is *Emmanuel*, 'God with us' (Isaiah 7:10-15; Matthew 1:23). His garments are suffused with light, a sign of the divinity concealed within him.

Within his halo, we see the Greek word for being, *Ho On*, the translation of the ineffable name that God revealed to Moses: 'I am who I am', or, 'I will be who I will be', expressing God's identity as the faithful and unchanging One (Exodus 3:14). This unspeakable name of God belongs by right to the little child in this icon, who is none other than the pre-existent God, revealed in time: but it will not be fully manifested until, after his death and resurrection, when he receives the name which is above all other names (Philippians 2:9).

In the Roman liturgy during the Christmas season, the church makes poetry of these wonderful paradoxes, singing:

Mary has given birth to a king, whose name is the eternal One. Uniting a mother's joy to the honour of virginity, this has never happened before nor will it ever happen again, alleluia!

(Antiphon from the Roman Rite feast of the Mother of God.)

Mary too has her mission and is ready to carry out her task. She holds her child with tenderness but does not cling to him. With her other hand she gestures to him as the Lamb of sacrifice whom all must worship. Her task is to bring him forth and let him go, to show him to the world as God incarnate and then, like his eternal Father, to hand him over to the power of sinners.

Intimacy must yield to exposition if the plan of God is to be revealed. The love of human motherhood must be transformed through the mystery of redemptive love into obedience to the mission willed by God. This is the mystery of Christ and Mary: obedience unto death and the discipleship that it demands. For him it leads to resurrection; for her it means that she becomes by grace the new Eve, the Mother of all who live.

Prayers before the Icon of the Tender Mother of God

We venerate your holy icon with love, O Virgin mother. We bow down in faith before you, proclaiming you to be the true Mother of God. Guard and protect us always, driving all danger far away from us.
(Byzantine prayer for the first Sunday in Lent, adapted.)

When she saw you on the cross, O Christ our God, the Creator of all, the Virgin Mother cried out in grief: 'O my Son, where has your beauty gone? I cannot bear to see you, unjustly hang upon the cross! Arise quickly that I may see your resurrection on the third day!'
(Byzantine prayer for Holy and Great Friday, adapted.)

Lord Jesus Christ, through the prayers of your most pure mother, have mercy on me a sinner!
Lord Jesus Christ, through the prayers of your most pure mother, have mercy on the human race!
Lord Jesus Christ, through the prayers of your most pure mother, fill the world with the light of the resurrection.

Three Icons of Mary as the *Hodegetria*, or the
One Who Shows the Way

(A)

A Meditation on three Icons of Mary as the *Hodegetria*, or the One Who Shows the Way

His mother said to the servants, 'Do whatever he tells you.'
(John 2:5)

As the continuation of her role in bringing the Word of God into the world, Mary's chief service to the church is to witness to Christ as the Saviour sent by God. These three icons show her in this role. The icon without an *oklad*, or metal cover, (A) belongs to the type known as the Mother of God from Kazan, the Russian city particularly associated with it. The brightly painted icon, from Ethiopia, (B) is the centre of a triptych with saints. The other (C) shows her pointing to Christ. Mary's whole being is a gesture of humility and obedience, a pointing away from herself. This was already shown in her Magnificat, recorded in St Luke's gospel (Luke 1:49), where she sings, 'The Mighty One has done great things for me and holy is his name', but it is also typical of what we are told about her in the fourth gospel as well. She directs people to do what Jesus tells them (John 2:5) and stands as a silent witness at the foot of the cross (John 19:25-27).

In these three icons of the *Hodegetria,* Mary shows us Christ who, according to St John (14:4-6) called himself the *hodos*, or way to the Father. In Christ, as the author of the letter to the Colossians tells us, 'are hidden all the treasures of wisdom and knowledge' (Colossians 2:3), since he is the one in whom the fullness of the Godhead dwells bodily (Colossians 2:9). At the last supper, the apostle Philip asked Jesus to show him the Father but Jesus restrained his desire for high-flying spiritual knowledge by simply pointing to himself as the locus of the Godhead:

Have I been with you all this time, Philip, and you still do not know me? Whoever has seen me has seen the Father. How can you say, 'Show us the Father?' Do you not believe that I am in the Father and the Father is in me? The words that I say to you I do not speak on my own; but the Father who dwells in me does his works. (John 14: 9-11)

However, it is important to recognise that Jesus too points toward himself not to draw attention to himself. It is in order to transcend himself in love for the one who sent him. He points to the Father who is revealed through him. Such a stance is typical of Jesus. He did not grasp at being equal with the Father in the unity of the Godhead (Philippians 2:6-7) and he translated this attitude of eternal self-abnegation into humility and obedience when he became incarnate on the earth:

Those who speak on their own seek their own glory: but the one who seeks the glory of him who sent him is true, and there is nothing false in him. (John 7:18)

Mary, the perfect disciple, in pointing to Jesus is therefore the living icon of Jesus himself as he points to the Father. She carries out her mission like her Son, in humility and obedience. This is the spiritual attitude depicted in these icons by her pointing hand and her exposition of the Christ child for us to contemplate. Attention that focuses too much on Mary herself is misguided. Her pointing hand reminds us that the preaching and witnessing of the church should have no other content than Jesus the Saviour of the world. He alone is the holy one, but he too aims our gaze not simply at himself, but at the One whose love he comes to bring us: his eternal Father.

(B)

(C)

Prayers before the Icons of Mary as *Hodegetria*

Calling to mind our all-holy, sinless, most blessed and glorious Lady, the Mother of God, and ever-virgin Mary, let us commit ourselves, and one another, and all our life to Christ our God!
(Byzantine prayer commemorating Mary)

Let us magnify the Mother of God, the Mother of the light!
It is truly right to praise you, all blessed and immaculate *Theotokos*, the Mother of our God! You are higher than the Cherubim and incomparably more glorious than the Seraphim, for without sin you have given birth to God the Word. True bearer of God, we magnify you!
(Byzantine hymns to the Theotokos, adapted)

Lord Jesus Christ, by the prayers of your most pure Mother, purify the eyes of our hearts to see the mysteries of the Father's kingdom!
Lord Jesus Christ, by the prayers of your most pure Mother, open our inner ears to receive your word!
Lord Jesus Christ, by the prayers of your most pure Mother, send the Holy Spirit to guide us into the truth!

What shall we call you, O most favoured one? Heaven, because the sun of righteousness has shown forth through you? Paradise, because your have made the bloom of incorruptibility to spring up? Virgin, because you have remained the undefiled one? Pure Mother, because you have given birth to your Son, the God of all things? O pray to him for us that he may save our souls!
(Byzantine prayer to the Mother of God)

A Meditation on the Icon of Christ's Baptism

The voice of the Lord is over the waters;
the God of glory thunders, the Lord, over mighty waters.
(Psalm 29: 3)

Although the baptism of Jesus is recorded in all three synoptic gospels (Mark 1:9-11; Matthew 3:13-17; Luke 3:21-22) and alluded to in that of St John (1:29-34), it has had a greater significance for the Christians of the East than for those in the West. In the Eastern churches, the event is celebrated on 6 January as one of the most solemn feasts of the entire year. It is known as the *Theophany,* or manifestation of God.

In the corresponding Western Christian feast, the Epiphany, although the emphasis falls mainly on the visit of the Magi to the infant Jesus (Matthew 2:1-16), there are some references to three great wonders celebrated on this day. The other two are Christ's baptism, and his first miracle at Cana in Galilee, when he transformed water into wine (John 2:1-11).

In the reforms following the Second Vatican Council, the Roman Catholic Church, recognising that such a major event in the life of Christ and in salvation history deserved more attention, improved the situation by establishing a feast of the baptism of Jesus to conclude the cycle of the Christmas season. However, it still does not mean much to many Catholics, as it can seem obscure in a context where baptism is often narrowly related to sin. Why did Jesus, the sinless one, need to be baptised at all?

The Eastern feast of the *Theophany,* is by contrast, dedicated to his baptism alone. It is a rich resource for understanding this event in the mission of Jesus, the incarnate Word.

The icon shows the moment of his baptism. Jesus is immersed in the waters of the Jordan, as the *Prodromos* or forerunner, John the Baptist, pours water over his head. On either side, angels wait to minister to him as he emerges from the river after his baptismal washing. In the Byzantine Rite, the event is celebrated as the original feast of the Holy Trinity.

It is a true *Theophany*, or manifestation of God. For a brief moment the veil before the Godhead is drawn aside and we are given access to the secret, inner life of God revealed through the appearance of the Son and Holy Spirit. One of the Byzantine hymns for the feast sets the tone for the whole celebration:

When you O Lord were baptised in the Jordan,
the worship of the Trinity was made manifest.
The voice of the Father bore witness to you by calling you
the beloved son.
The Spirit in the form of a dove confirmed his word as true.
O Christ our God, who appeared and gave light to the
world, glory be to you!
(Hymn from the feast of the Holy Theophany in the
Byzantine Office of Great Compline.)

But exalted as this revelation is, the question still remains: why did Jesus come to be baptised? Three reasons emerge from the celebration of the feast and each reveals a new layer of meaning. Firstly, the incarnate Word sanctifies water, the primal element from which all life has come, by going down into the waters of the river Jordan. This cosmic aspect of the mystery, God entering into creation to sanctify it, speaks especially to many contemporary Christians who concern themselves with ecological issues.

Secondly, his descent into the water points forward to that greater descent he will accomplish in the future, when he goes down into the grave, passes through the gates of hell on Holy Saturday, and descends into the realm of the dead in Hades.

Thirdly, his baptism is the first public occasion for the appearance of the Holy Spirit who accompanies him at every point in his ministry and anoints him to become the promised Christ. There is an essential reciprocity between the mission of the eternal Son as redeemer and the mission of the Holy Spirit as sanctifier. Both work together in the revelation of the Father and the salvation of the world.

Jesus did not *become* the Son of God at his baptism, as some heretical groups in the early church believed, but his divine Sonship, veiled behind the form of a servant, was revealed for the first time to the eyes of faith. It was the descent of the Holy Spirit that openly declared Jesus to be the Messiah. His baptism was the solemn moment of commissioning when he was shown to be the suffering servant of God, the high priest, who by offering his life in sacrifice would take away the sins of the world (John 1:36). The anointed one became the appointed one, appointed to act on behalf of sinful humanity with his heavenly Father (Hebrews 5:5-6). St Luke records the interesting detail that Jesus received the Holy Spirit as he was praying after his baptism. He hints in this way that the baptism marked a new stage in the human self-awareness of the incarnate Son of God (Luke 3:21-22) who had to grow in wisdom in his human nature (Luke 2:52).

After this event, St Mark says that the Spirit drove Jesus out into the wilderness, to the place of temptation (Mark 1:12), where he began the war with Satan that would culminate in his triumph on the cross. St Luke depicts him after the temptation in the desert, returning to Nazareth where he had been brought up and declaring in the Synagogue in words from the prophet Isaiah:

> *The Spirit of the Lord is upon me because he has anointed*
> *me to bring good news to the poor.*
> *He has sent me to proclaim release to the captives*
> *and recovery of sight to the blind,*
> *to let the oppressed go free,*
> *to proclaim the year of the Lord's favour.*

(Luke 4:18-19, quoting from Isaiah 61:1-2.)

Sometimes, Christians can have a somewhat deficient understanding of the Holy Spirit's work. They may forget the Spirit's unique role in salvation and his infinite sovereignty as the third person of the Holy Trinity. This kind of forgetfulness can result in an over-emphasis on the church as body and institution, engendering an excessively external understanding of relationship with Christ. Life in Christ, the purpose of our baptism, can easily degenerate into a superficial imitation of him.

On the other hand, an exaggerated emphasis on the experience of the Spirit without explicit reference to Christ, due discretion or even common sense, can cut off the believer from the incarnate truth of Christ, denying the reality not only of the flesh and blood of Jesus, but of the human aspects of the church and sacraments in which he wishes us to meet him (1 John 5:6-9). The result may be a kind of immaturity, too dependent on the need for enthusiastic experiences. Both tendencies can lead to an unbalanced spirituality.

The mystery of Christ's baptism depicted in this icon is a powerful reminder that the Son and Spirit are like the two hands of God by means of which he shapes and saves the world. An authentic Christian spirituality calls for a healthy balance between the incarnate Word (institution) and the charisms of the Spirit (event). There is a legitimate place to be accorded to both experience and authority.

Finally, it reminds us that Christ and the Holy Spirit have been *sent* to us by God! They are the supreme gifts who have appeared to draw us upwards to the person of the sender: the Father, the source and origin of creation and of grace. This is one of the most penetrating insights in the Eastern Christian understanding of grace: God does not give us gifts that are separate from him. He gives *himself* to us.

Prayers before the Icon of Christ's Baptism

John the Baptist cried aloud as he saw the Lamb of God who takes away the sins of the world: 'In your mercy Lord, sanctify me and give me light. You are the life, the light and the peace of all the world!'
(Byzantine hymn for the feast of the Theophany, adapted.)

When you went down into the waters and crushed the head of the dragon, you gave light to all. Let us glorify you our Saviour, who give illumination to our hearts.
(Byzantine hymn for the feast of the Theophany, adapted.)

Almighty, ever-living God, we are your children, born again of water and the Holy Spirit. May we live from the fullness of your Spirit in our hearts, through Christ our Lord. Amen.
(Roman Rite prayer from the feast of the Baptism of Jesus, adapted.)

Lord Jesus, by the mystery of your baptism, and the prayers of the holy forerunner John, enlighten my mind with the knowledge of the Trinity!
Lord Jesus, by the light of your baptism, take away the sin of the world!
Lord Jesus, by your descent into the waters of the Jordan, make holy your whole creation and help us to recognise in it the gift of your love!

Icon of the Crucifixion

A Meditation on the Icon of the Crucifixion

Praise him, sun and moon; praise him, all you shining stars!
(Psalm 148:3)

In the Eastern churches, the depiction of Jesus on the cross is strongly influenced by the presentation of the crucifixion in St John's gospel. Despite his agony, the crucified Saviour radiates serenity, a dignity in death. All is calm, and still: there are usually no tortured figures of Jesus in the form to which Western Christians are accustomed. Emotion when it is expressed is restrained and dignified, for it is the incarnate God who suffers on the cross, the sinless one for sinners that he might bring us back to God (1 Peter 3:18).

Although Eastern liturgical texts and spiritual writers take the reality of his sufferings in deadly earnest, the iconographers draw a veil of sacred reticence over depicting them too explicitly in art. The mystery is too awesome, too elevated, to be shown in merely human terms. In addition, like the gospels themselves, the crucifixion is bathed in the light of Easter Sunday. Orthodoxy never forgets that the one who hung upon the cross and went down into the deepest depths of the earth, is also the risen one (Ephesians 4:8-11). His resurrection does not cancel or diminish the reality of his sufferings but on the contrary testifies to the unity of God's plan, since Christ was put to death for our sins and raised for our justification.

This icon faithfully reflects the Orthodox tradition. All the central actors in the drama are there: the beloved disciple with Mary the *Theotokos*, Mary Magdalene and the Centurion (John 19:25-27). The Mother of God shows her deep emotion by her posture. But as in those icons where she carries the Christ child, she also performs her mission of pointing to her Son upon the cross. The city walls, in the background of the picture, suggest the holy city Jerusalem, for Christ enduring his passion, suffered as an outcast, beyond the city gates (Hebrews 13:12-13). On either side of the cross the sponge and spear are standing, representing the piercing of the Saviour's side and the vinegar he was offered (John 19:28-38).

The slight curvature of the panel heightens the sense that the figure on the cross is moving out towards us: Christ's crucifixion breaks out of the time and space in which it happened. It is an event of cosmic and eternal significance that reaches out into the future, into all time and space. So, around the central image stand the saints who have shared by grace in the passion of Christ in their own lives.

The top and bottom of the icon tell us much about the spiritual meaning of this terrible event, which is yet the working out of a divine plan. The foot of the cross pierces the hill of Golgotha, but beneath it lies a black space. Within the space we see a skull, a symbol evoking numerous associations. It represents Calvary, the place of the skull. It is in addition a reminder of mortality from which we will be rescued by the Lord's self-offering on the cross. It also calls to mind an early Christian tradition, not literally or historically true but true in the world of iconographical symbolism, that Jesus the new Adam was crucified over the corpse of the old Adam, our fallen proto-parent, the source of all humanity's ills.

Death and decay, our human condition, are thus transformed by the new Adam, who suffered on the cross to bring life and hope to humankind. The two Adams, one earthly, the other heavenly, meet on the common ground of suffering and mortality (1 Corinthians 15:20-28; 42-49). The black space pierced by the foot of the cross suggests the abyss of nothingness above which human existence is suspended by the creative word of God. As a sign of this nothingness out of which God made all things, it is an awesome reminder of what creation means: that all is empty without the constant support of God.

At the top of the icon, to the left and right, the sun and moon are shown. The early Christian vision of the cross (reflected in the ancient Latin hymns still sung in Benedictine monastic worship) was strongly cosmic in its emphasis:

Sing my tongue of warfare ended,
Of the Victor's laurelled crown;
Let the cross his trophy splendid,
Be the theme of high renown;
How a broken world was mended –
Life restored by life laid down.

Gall he drinks; his strength subduing,
Reed and thorn and nail and spear
Plot his gentle frame's undoing;
Blood and water thence appear,
With their cleansing tide renewing
Earth and sea and starry sphere!

Jesus died on the cross not simply to save individuals. On the contrary the cross was like a great tree of life spreading its branches over the face of the earth:

'By a tree the race reprieving
Whom a tree long since betrayed.'
(Hymn by Venantius Fortunatus, in the Good Friday liturgy of the Roman Rite.)

By means of its fruit which is salvation, this tree of life redeems the tree of Eden which had borne its terrible fruit of sin and death (Genesis 3:1-22). The roots of this tree of life, the cross, reach down into the black realm of death and nothingness, but its branches spread up and outwards to embrace the universe. It reaches up towards the very sun, moon and stars, as God remakes the shattered cosmos through his Son's redeeming blood.

This icon is a powerful symbol of the all-embracing love of Christ. It reminds us, as the Roman liturgy for Easter night puts it, that if God's love was wonderful in first creating the world, then it was incomparably more wonderful in re-creating it after it had fallen. It sets before us the providential plan of love:

> *How a broken world was mended –*
> *Life restored by life laid down.*

Prayers before the Icon of the Crucifixion

Today the one who hung the earth upon the waters is
    hung upon the cross.
The one who is the king of angels receives a crown of
    thorns.
The one who wraps the heavens with cloud is wrapped in
the purple cloak of mockery.
The one who set Adam free by his baptism in the Jordan
    is struck upon the face.
The bridegroom of the church is pierced with nails.
The son of the Virgin is pierced with a lance.
We venerate your passion O Christ!
Let us see as well your glorious resurrection!

Having beheld the resurrection of Christ, let us worship
    the holy Lord Jesus, the only sinless one!
Your cross, O Christ, we venerate!
Your holy resurrection we glorify!
You are our God and we know no other.
We call upon your name!

Come all people and let us worship the holy resurrection
of Christ. For see, because of the tree, joy has come into
the whole world!

Therefore blessing the Lord in everything, we sing his
resurrection, for by suffering the cross for us, he has
destroyed death by his death!
(Hymns from the Byzantine Rite for the Holy and Great Week.)

O Christ who fashioned Eve from Adam's side! From your
pierced side flow rivers of cleansing water. From out of
your side, a double stream flowed forth: in drinking from
it we have received eternal life!
*(Hymn from the Byzantine Office for Holy and Great Friday
evening.)*

Lord Jesus, crucified for my sins, have mercy on me!
Lord Jesus, open your arms and receive the suffering of
    the world!
Lord Jesus, let us die to sin and rise to life with you!

The Mystery of Death and Resurrection:
The Diptych of Christ's Descent into Hades and Mary's *Koimesis*, or *Dormition*.

Where, O death is your victory? Where, O death is your sting?
(1 Corinthians 15:55)

This portable, folding icon depicts the mystery of death and resurrection, shown in the victory of Christ and the glorification of his Mother. Christ is depicted in the event known to Western Christians as the 'harrowing of hell', that is, his descent into the underworld. Mary is shown in her 'falling asleep', that is, her *koimesis*, or *dormition* as Jesus comes to receive her soul.

A Meditation on the Icon of Christ's Descent into Hades

> For you do not give me up to Sheol,
> or let your faithful one see the pit.
> (Psalm 16:10)

In the Eastern churches, the descent of Christ into Hades, or the unseen world, to proclaim salvation to all who waited for the good news, represents the culmination of his saving work and the triumph of life over death and sin (1 Peter 3:18-20). It is the dawn of the resurrection.

This icon shows the Lord Jesus, resplendent in a *mandorla*, an almond-shaped halo of light, signifying both his divinity and the glory of the resurrection. It encompasses his whole body as he arrives in the underworld after his terrible death on the cross. It is 'Holy-Saturday time and space'. He comes to rescue Adam and Eve, the proto-parents of the human race and to announce salvation to the prophets and kings of old, who are shown waiting for the long-desired Redeemer. Under his feet lie the gates of hell, trampled down in victory. Scattered round about are the instruments of torture by means of which Satan had tormented the human race. So the Roman liturgy sings in triumph on Holy Saturday:

> *Our Shepherd, the source of living water has gone away. At his passing the one who held the first man captive is a captive now himself. Today our Saviour has shattered the bars and broken down the gates of death. He has pulled down the barricades of hell and overthrown Satan's power.*

(Roman Rite text for Holy Saturday Matins)

The Redeemer carries out in his own life the promise he had made to his disciples: 'The one who endures to the end will be saved' (Matthew 24:13). Christ went to the bitter end in solidarity with the human race in death. This was his hour of total stripping, the culmination of the descent that began when he emptied himself, assumed the condition of a slave and in humility accepted death, even death on a cross (Philippians 2:8). As he illuminated the darkness of the underworld with the light of resurrection, the lamentations of Good Friday and the deathly silence of Holy Saturday were transformed into the jubilant Alleluia of the paschal feast.

The icon shows the victory of life over death, of hope over despair, as Jesus calls Adam and Eve out of the underworld and lifts them up to everlasting life. As in the crucifixion icon, we see the meeting of the two Adams, but this time there is no more suffering, no more death. The redeemer has brought the human race to life again.

What a marvellous paradox! This icon of descent or, *katabasis*, the ultimate descent into the deepest darkness of the grave and the underworld, is at the same time the icon of ascent, *anastasis*, the resurrection of Christ into life without end.

His glorious resurrection is the flaming heart of the Christian gospel, the transformation of death into abundant, endless life. That is why the Byzantine liturgy proclaims on Holy Saturday night:

Now are all things filled with light,

and why the Roman Church prays on Easter night:

This is the night when Jesus Christ snapped the chains of death and rose in triumph from the grave!

Prayers before the Icon of Christ's Descent into Hades

'O Light of Christ rising in glory, scatter the darkness of
our hearts and minds!'
(Prayer from the Roman Rite Paschal Vigil.)

I am counted among those who go down to the Pit;
I am like those who have no help,
like those forsaken among the dead,
like the slain that lie in the grave,
like those whom you remember no more,
for they are cut off from your hand.
You have put me in the depths of the pit,
in the regions dark and deep.

Every day I call on you O Lord;
I spread out my hands to you.
(from Psalm 88)

Christ has risen from the dead, trampling down death by
death, and on those in the tombs bestowing life.
(Byzantine hymn for Paschal time.)

Let us see, O Lord, the light of your holy resurrection as
we sing, 'Glory to your passion, O Christ!'
(Text from the Glenstal Monastic Office for Holy Saturday.)

Lord Jesus our light, who descended to the dead, give
    light to all who sit in darkness and in the shadow of
    death!
Lord Jesus our light, who went down into the gloom of
    hell, release all souls from the hell of loneliness and
    lack of love!
Lord Jesus our light, source of everlasting love, lift up all
    creation to the praise and glory of the Father!

A Meditation on the Icon of
Mary's *Koimesis* or *Dormition*

Rise up, O Lord, and go to your resting place,
you and the ark of your might.
(Psalm132:8)

The icon of Mary's *koimesis*, or *dormition*, her falling asleep, shows us the moment when Christ came to receive her soul at the end of her life. The event is not recorded in holy scripture but is largely based on a traditional account by St Dionysios the Areopagite, who claimed to have been a witness to it. He tells us that the apostles, who are shown gathered around Mary's bier, had been miraculously assembled to witness the moment when her Son came to take his mother's soul to heaven.

Eastern Christian teaching on Mary rarely separates her from the other actors in the Christian drama, either from Jesus, or from the church in which she is the first of the redeemed. Here, as she returns to God, she is shown as at the Ascension and at Pentecost, surrounded by the apostles. The risen Lord Jesus, shining with the *mandorla*, the light of his resurrection glory, holds his mother's soul like a newly born infant, wrapped in swaddling clothes.

So he had himself been held in swaddling bands by Mary his mother at Bethlehem in the night of Christmas (Luke 2:6-7) and then, stripped naked at the foot of the cross, when she received his body for burial. The message of the icon is clear: Jesus is, in the order of grace, like a mother through whom we are born again into eternal life. Mary is the faithful witness to Jesus. She is the disciple in whom he carries out his work. With the Orthodox Church, and the whole Eastern Christian world, the Roman Catholic Church too confesses her glorification after death, revering her as the great sign that appears in heaven, the woman clothed with the sun, standing on the moon and crowned with the stars to guide us on our pilgrim way to God (Revelation 12:1-17).

Prayers before the Icon of Mary's *Dormition*

You would not permit decay to touch her mortal body for she had given birth to your Son, the Lord of all life, in the glory of the incarnation.
(From the Roman Rite Preface for the feast of the Assumption.)

Mary has been taken up to heaven, the angels are rejoicing. Together they sing for joy and praise the Lord, proclaiming, 'Alleluia.'
(From the Roman Rite Office of Lauds for the feast of the Assumption.)

O Virgin Mother of God,
Rejoice so highly favoured!
The Lord is with you.
Blessed are you among women and blessed is the fruit of your womb,
For you have given birth to the Saviour of our souls.
In you I place all my hope O Mother of God.
Guard me under your protection.
(Byzantine prayer to the Mother of God)

Powers, thrones and principalities,
Cherubim and awesome Seraphim
glorify your *dormition*, and those on earth who are
adorned by your glory rejoice.

They say, with kings, angels and archangels,
'Hail full of grace! The Lord is with you,
granting great mercy to the world, through you.'
(Hymn for the Byzantine feast of the Dormition, adapted.)

Lord Jesus, by the mystery of your Mother's *dormition*
    awaken us from the sleep of death!
Lord Jesus, by the mystery of your Mother's *dormition*
    wipe away the tears of all who mourn!
Lord Jesus, by the mystery of your Mother's *dormition*, fill
    us with the hope of resurrection!

A Meditation on the Icon of
Christ's Ascension into Heaven

*As they were watching, he was lifted up, and a cloud took
him out of their sight.*
(Acts 1:9)

The celebration of the mystery of the ascension developed
liturgically in the Eastern churches as a dramatic commemoration of the final event in the history of Christ's
saving deeds on behalf of the world. The event itself is
recorded in the so-called longer ending of St Mark's gospel
(16:19-20), but it is also implied in that of St Matthew
(28:16-20). St Luke is the one who provides the most
detailed account, both at the end of his gospel (Luke 24:50-
53) and in the opening chapter of the Acts of the Apostles
(1:1-14). St John's gospel does not contain such a record,
because with his characteristically unitary understanding
of the work of Jesus, John sees his glorification as a single
action, beginning with his lifting up on the cross (12:32)
and culminating in his resurrection.

However, the church's liturgical wisdom, in its desire to
celebrate the mysteries of Jesus, has followed the Lucan
account since it allows for a distinct event in which the
work of redemption culminates. At the last supper John
records that Jesus promised the coming of another *Paraclete* (comforter or counsellor) whom the Father would
send in his name (John 14:15; 26). For this reason, he says,
it is to the disciples' advantage that he should return to
the Father (John 16:7) so that the Holy Spirit may come
to them.

St Luke takes up this close connection between the departure of Jesus and the arrival of the Holy Spirit, a connection expressed also in the various liturgical traditions of Christianity, East and West. Indeed he tells us that just before his ascension, the Lord commanded his disciples to wait in Jerusalem until the promised Spirit would come (Acts 1:4-5).

The tradition of the church has discerned three deep truths in the mystery of Christ's ascension. The first we find emphasised in the letter to the Ephesians: Christ has ascended on high so as to become the head of his body the church and to fill all things with his presence (Ephesians 1: 20-23). The author sees the ascension as the end of the trajectory traced by Jesus in his act of self-emptying, which led to the cross and the descent to the dead. Christ has received the fullness of grace as head, so as to pour it out on his body the church (Ephesians 4:7-10):

> But each of us was given grace according to the measure of Christ's gift. Therefore it is said, 'When he ascended on high, he made captivity itself a captive; he gave gifts to his people.' (When it says, 'He ascended', what does it mean but that he had also descended into the lower parts of the earth? He who descended is the same one who ascended far above all the heavens, so that he might fill all things.)

The letter observes that all the gifts of ministry given by the ascended Christ to the church enable the whole body to grow up to the stature of its glorified Lord.

The second truth contained in this mystery is similar to the first. It concerns Christ's continuing work as mediator of the new covenant and is particularly emphasised in the letter to the Hebrews. In heaven at the right hand of God the Father, the risen Jesus exercises his priestly ministry, interceding for the sins of the people and pleading his completed sacrifice in the presence of the Father (Hebrews 5-9). Liturgical tradition (including that of Rome) frequently mentions an altar on high where this priesthood is carried out. Jesus has lifted up the sacrifice of love he accomplished on the cross and carried it back into its source in the circle of love within the Trinity.

The third truth emerges by reflecting on the scene of the ascension itself as we see it depicted here. The icon shows the company of the disciples gathered beneath the ascended Lord. He is radiant in the glory of heaven where he is attended upon by angels. In the centre stands Mary the *Theotokos* with her hands crossed in prayer. She too is accompanied by angels, 'men in white' as the scriptural account names them, who speak to the disciples. In many icons the group of apostles includes not only Peter but also Paul. By including Mary and Paul, the icon shows that the ascension is not just a commemoration of a past event, but

an icon of the church which is about to be born through the descent of the Spirit at Pentecost.

The ascension is the mystery by which the historically conditioned events of the life of Jesus received their perpetual validity for us. By enthroning our humanity – the instrument by means of which he carried out our redemption – at the right hand of the Father, Christ has, in the words of the Roman liturgy, 'given our mortal nature immortal worth'. Thanks to his ascension, the events of his life and death become for us, in the power of the Holy Spirit, a fountain of life and grace in the church until he comes again in glory. It is therefore the basis of our worship and our future glorification. Where Christ our head has gone in glory, there we, the body, are called in hope.

However, it is not enough for the church simply to accept this passively, gazing in unbroken contemplation after her departing Lord. The angels ask (Acts 1:11),

Men of Galilee, why do you stand looking up toward heaven?
This Jesus who has been taken up away from you into heaven,
will come in the same way as you saw him go into heaven.

The implications are clear. There is no time to simply stand and gaze. The church like Mary of Bethany (Luke 10:38-40) must never lose sight of her heavenly Lord (Hebrews 12:2). But at the same time she is not called to passivity or inertia. Like Jesus, Christians must allow themselves to be driven by the Spirit (Mark 1:12). They are called to be apostles, to proclaim the good news of God's redeeming love. That is the task of Christ's disciples in the time between the ascension and the second coming.

Prayers before the Icon of the Ascension

O King of glory and Lord of hosts who ascended in triumph today above all the heavens: do not leave us orphaned but send to us the promise of the Father, the Holy Spirit of truth, alleluia.

(Roman Rite antiphon for the feast of the Ascension)

Be exalted, O God, above the heavens. Let your glory be over all the earth. (Psalm 57: 5)

Lord Jesus Christ you are seated at the right hand of the
    Father: receive our prayer!
Lord Jesus Christ, you ascended on high: send us the Holy
    Spirit!
Lord Jesus Christ in the glory of the Father: lead us on the
    way to God's kingdom!

Let God arise, let his enemies be scattered,
let those who hate him flee before him.
Sing to God, sing praises to his name;
lift up a song to him who rides upon the clouds –
his name is the Lord – be exultant before him.
(Psalm 68:1, 4)

Make our minds ascend O Lord to the place of your
    dwelling and our hearts to the meeting place of your
    majesty.
May our rise thoughts to the contemplation of your
    glory:
and grant that we may honour with fitting praises
this illustrious mystery of your ascension,
and give glory to your Father and to the Holy Spirit.
(Hymn from the Syrian tradition)

A Meditation on the Icon of St Nicholas

Be merciful, just as your Father is merciful.
(Luke 6:36)

The vibrant red in this icon symbolises the fire and energy of the Holy Spirit. It reminds us that every icon involves both evocation and invocation. Evocation because it calls to mind the saint depicted. Here it is Nicholas of Myra, beloved of mariners and children from Russia to the coast of Galway. Nicholas, guide of sailors, giver of gifts and patron saint of generosity. Every icon is an evocation because it is a reminder that the saints who opened their hearts to God's transforming grace became themselves living icons of the crucified and risen Jesus. He is the perfect icon of God (Colossians 1:15-20; 2 Corinthians 4:4), 'the reflection of God's glory and the exact imprint of God's very being' (Hebrews 1:3).

St Nicholas is shown here with his features transformed by holiness. His deep-set, compassionate eyes gaze contemplatively upon the believer. His high forehead reveals his great wisdom. It is surrounded by a nimbus or halo symbolising the light of grace. His expression is one of deep serenity, the inner tranquillity of one who keeps the Lord ever in his sight (Psalm 16:8-9).

In every true icon, light emerges from within the person, from the deep well of the sanctified heart. It is there that the Holy Spirit infuses the light of baptismal grace, called by the ancient church, both East and West, *Photismos*, or illumination. This light comes down from on high from the Father of all light (James 1:17). It is the light that shone through the body of Christ on Thabor, the mount of Transfiguration, and that shines forever through his risen body (Matthew 17:1-10; 2 Peter 1:16-18). This light of love is poured into the heart of the believer by baptism in the Holy Spirit (Romans 5:5), into the unconscious centre of the person. It calls out from within, until turning inwards in prayer, the seeker sees and knows it in conscious experience (Romans 6:1-4). The saint is one who has made this experience his or her own.

Flanking Nicholas on either side are Christ the Lord, and Mary the *Theotokos*. Their presence indicates that his strength came from heaven above, from the grace of the Saviour and the prayers of Mary, Mother of the Church. She presents him with his *omphorion* or stole, a potent reminder that ministry is given by the church for the service of others. Nicholas wears the vestments in which he carried out his ministry before the Lord. All is evocation, a reminder that God's favour rests upon Nicholas his chosen witness.

His special virtue was compassion, which is written in his face. Orthodox spirituality has always seen the gift of tears as the purest sign of union with God. They are tears of repentance, tears of compassion and tears of joy, tokens of that tenderness of heart without which one can never see the Lord. Nicholas has always had a prominent place in popular devotion, especially in the Christian East. A Russian proverb says that even if God himself were to die, at least we would have St Nicholas!

But if the icon is an evocation, it is still more an invocation. It is a privileged place, a locus for the sacred, where the Holy Spirit shines in answer to our prayers. The painter of this icon, an anonymous servant, has put his art at the disposal of the vision he received in prayer. He has received the impression of a heavenly 'original', obscurely sensed in the darkness of contemplative prayer and worship.

Expressing it in wood and paint and gold, he has fashioned the likeness of the saint. Since his prayer was pure, the material elements have caught 'fire' from the uncreated light. This icon of Nicholas shines with a holiness not of this world. It reveals to the eyes of faith and prayer the mysterious vocation to which all are called in baptism – to catch 'fire' in turn from the divine light. 'Come and receive light from the undying light of Christ,' sings the Byzantine liturgy in the holy night of Easter. The Holy Spirit, the 'breath of God' will fan this tiny flame into a bonfire of love if the heart is repeatedly opened to him in prayer.

In the sayings of the desert monks we read that a young man asked an elder what else he needed do in his spiritual life, since he kept the round of prayers and duties appointed for him to the best of his ability. The old man stood up, stretched out his hands to heaven, shone like the sun and said, 'If you want to, you can become fire!'

The undying light that kindles this fire is the joyful light of Thabor. It shone before the eyes of Peter, James and John in the event of the Transfiguration (Mark 9:1-9) and in the holy life of Nicholas. It shone in the eyes of the painter who perceived his presence in pure prayer. This light can shine for us today, in the silent, receptive space we make within ourselves as we pray before the icon of St Nicholas.

Submit to the light: then the gentle compassion of this saint will be yours as well. God wishes to shed his light in human hearts to make them shine like living icons before the face of all the earth (Matthew 5:14-16).

Your saints shall dwell in everlasting glory! An immortal
name will be their heritage!
(Antiphon from the Glenstal Monastic Office.)

Lord Jesus Christ, Son of the living God, by the prayers of
    your servant Nicholas grant us a childlike heart to
    know and do your will!
Lord Jesus Christ, gentle and humble in heart, pour out
    on us the spirit of mercy and compassion!
Lord Jesus Christ, fill with love and understanding the
    hearts we lift up to you in prayer!

Grant almighty God, that by means of our prayer to your
servant Nicholas, you may increase our love and further
our salvation, through Christ our Lord. Amen.
(Prayer from the Roman Rite Office for Confessors.)

Almighty God, listen to our prayers for mercy. In your
goodness, grant us the help of St Nicholas. By his
intercession protect us from all dangers and guide us on
our way to you, through Christ our Lord. Amen.
(Prayer from the Roman Rite, adapted)

We have seen the true light!
We have found the true faith!
We worship the undivided Trinity:
this has been our salvation!
(Byzantine hymn)

The Icon of Saints Basil, Gregory the Theologian and John Chrysostom

A Meditation on the Icon of Saints Basil, Gregory the Theologian and John Chrysostom

For we do not proclaim ourselves; we proclaim Jesus
Christ as Lord and ourselves as your slaves for Jesus' sake.

(2 Corinthians 4:5)

In the Orthodox tradition these three fathers of the church,
are often depicted together. This is a Greek icon showing
these outstanding teachers of Christian truth who lived in
the fourth and early fifth centuries, a period of great
turmoil in the life of the church. Two of them were close
friends. The Eastern church calls them, 'Great teachers of
the world', while the West has honoured them with the
title, 'Doctors of the Church.' On the left is Basil the Great
(330-379), in the centre is John Chrysostom (c.349-407), and
at the right is Gregory Nazianzen (330-c.390). These three
holy doctors have enlightened the church with heavenly
wisdom, but the light was not really theirs: it was only lent
to them for the good of God's people.

Therefore, above them the Lord Jesus hovers with
hands outstretched in blessing, to show that their wise
teaching comes from the one true teacher, the Christ. It
flows from him since he is the wisdom of God, and the
light pouring out from the eternal Father, the source of all
light. In the words of the apostle James, wisdom and light
come down from above (James 1:17-18; 3:17-18).

Each is dressed in the vestment of an Orthodox bishop,
embroidered with many crosses, the *polystaurion*, to signify
that they follow a crucified Lord, the true Shepherd who
laid down his life for his flock (John 10:11-18). Over their
shoulders is draped the *omphorion*, the festal stole, as a sign

that they bear the cross of Christ in the service of their flocks. Their right hands are raised in blessing, in the delicate, graceful gesture distinctive to the Greek Church, by which the person of Jesus is recalled even in the very fingers of the hand.

The gracefulness of their gestures demonstrates that their bodies have been refined by grace. They each hold a gospel book for they are teachers of Orthodox truth, communicating God's revelation contained in his word.

As bishops they are also high priests who lead their people in glorifying God in prayer and praise, since 'Orthodoxy' means *both* correct doctrine and correct worship.

But the saints, no matter how great, were still mortal beings and these three luminaries were no exception to this rule. It was precisely as weak and fallible mortals, as 'clay jars' (2 Corinthians 4:7-12) that they magnetically drew down the grace of God upon themselves and dispensed it to others. Basil was a great leader, a bishop and an administrator. He was also a legislator for monks, to whom later generations, including St Benedict, looked back as a pure and noble source of the monastic tradition. But we know from his correspondence with his friends that he was not always easy an easy person to deal with. He was a tough ecclesiastical politician who had to fight for the truth of Christ in difficult times, to prevent it's being watered down. He sometimes rode a little roughshod over others in his concern to uphold and protect the truth.

John was dubbed, *Chrysostomos*, or, 'the golden-mouthed', because of his rhetoric and the power of his preaching. He was especially effective in upholding the cause of the poor. The eucharistic prayer ascribed to his authorship is still a central text of the Byzantine liturgy to this day, and may very well derive in some measure from him. But his glorious preaching could be harsh.

Gregory is traditionally known in the East as, 'the theologian', a title he shares with the evangelist St John and the mystic St Symeon the New Theologian (949-1022). He received this title because he wrote inspired and beautiful hymns in praise of the Holy Trinity. But he was by nature inclined to hypersensitivity. He was not at all suited to the political turmoil of the church into which his friend Basil plunged him. Pastoral responsibility involved for him at times, severe inner suffering.

These three, Basil, Gregory and John, were flawed human beings, but they were also great lovers of God and seekers of the truth. By God's grace alone, since as the Roman liturgy puts it, 'he chooses the weak and strengthens them', they became shining lights of Orthodox truth and are praised together as the three holy hierarchs and teachers of the faith. We should pray to them to share their light with us, to help us penetrate the mysteries of the faith and to become true theologians. In an Eastern Christian perspective that means: to be consecrated to the contemplation of the Trinity and the mystery of Christ, in prayer and worship.

O Supreme Doctors and luminaries of the church, Basil, Gregory and John! O lovers of the law of God, pray for us to the Son of God.
(*Roman Rite antiphon for Vespers from the Common of Doctors of the Church, adapted.*)

O God of my ancestors and Lord of mercy,
who have made all things by your word,
and by your wisdom have formed humankind
to have dominion over the creatures you have made …
give me the wisdom that sits by your throne and do not
reject me from among your servants.

Send her forth from the holy heavens
and from the throne of your glory send her,
that she may labour at my side,
and that I may learn what is pleasing to you.
(*Prayer of King Solomon from Wisdom 9:1-4, 10*)

O Wisdom, you come forth from the mouth of the most high. Reaching from end to end, you sweetly but strongly dispose all things. O come and teach us the way of prudence.
(*Roman Rite antiphon for Advent*)

Lord Jesus, light of wisdom, teach us the wisdom that
    comes from above!
Lord Jesus light of truth, guide our feet on the way of
    peace!
Lord Jesus radiance of the Father's glory, lead us to our
    heavenly home!

A Meditation on the Icon of St Athanasius

Wisdom will exalt him above his neighbours,
and will open his mouth in the midst of the assembly.
(Sirach 15:5)

The personality of St Athanasius, Bishop of Alexandria, dominated the history of the early church. As the great defender of Christ's divinity against the Arian heresy, his interventions at and after the church's first universal council in 325, led to the definition that Christ is truly *homoousios*, or one in substance with the Father: 'God from God, light from light, true God from true God.' Thus he carried out a very public work, first as deacon and then as Bishop of Alexandria, in defending and proclaiming the full truth about Jesus.

On the other hand he was also keenly aware of the importance of the inner life in Christianity. As an admirer and supporter of the emerging Egyptian monasticism of his day, tradition credits him with writing the *Life of Anthony*, one of the earliest desert ascetics, who is venerated as the patriarch of monks. This book had enormous influence in the history of Christianity and contributed greatly to the growth of monasticism in the West. It was also instrumental in the conversion of St Augustine (354-430) as he related in his famous *Confessions*. Thus St Athanasius supported the inner life of prayer and contemplation, the source of all the church's apostolic fruitfulness, as vigorously as he worked for her mission in the world.

This icon shows him in his magisterial authority. He is seated on a *kathedra*, or throne, symbolising his teaching office. He holds an open book and wears liturgical vestments – the *phelonion*, or chasuble, *omophorion*, or stole, and the lozenge shaped ornament, the *epigonation*, that hangs at his side. His hand is raised in blessing.

The image is direct and pure, its stark frontality and gold background confronting the viewer with this powerful personality. It concentrates on the essentials only: the image of the saint displayed in his episcopal insignia. The gold background announces that he speaks to us from the transfigured life of heaven into which he has been taken up. It sets him firmly against the backdrop of eternity.

It is worth observing that this very Eastern icon, with its Greek inscription, reveals clear signs of Western influence. Despite its strongly Byzantine aspects, perspective is used in the painting of the throne and shading in the details of the costume.

The icon comes from a time and place (the post-Byzantine period), during which the Latin Catholics of Venice exercised authority in the Aegean islands. On Crete and in the Aegean area in general, despite the religious differences between the Latins and the Greeks, the members of both churches mixed, intermarried and mingled very freely. Indeed recent research has established the existence of a richly ecumenical culture – though not without tensions – which resulted in the 'westernisation' of the icon. That culture is reflected in this icon of St Athanasius.

There may have been an official split in the church, but these divided halves of Christendom lived and worked together, often sharing each other's pastoral ministrations. Contemporary Byzantine art historians, far from thinking that serious Greek iconography stopped after the fall of Constantinople to the Turks in 1453, now insist that many interesting and impressive icons date from this very period.

It was also a time when Orthodox spiritual writers such as the great Greek saint from the island of Naxos, Nikodemos the Hagiorite (1748-1809), adapted Latin Catholic writings (such as the *Spiritual Exercises* of St Ignatius Loyola), reshaping them in accordance with Eastern spiritual needs. Such an eclectic, mixed culture is an appropriate context within which an icon of St Athanasius would have been painted. In addition to being a father shared in common by both East and West, he received considerable support from the Roman church in defending the divinity of Jesus. He even lived for two years in Trier, now in Germany, where he was exiled for his beliefs.

In addition, Athanasius has a much wider significance. He is a saint not only for Catholics and Orthodox but also – perhaps especially – for the oriental Orthodox Copts of Egypt, his spiritual heirs. They are proud to call themselves his successors in the great church of Egypt. His icon is a sign of unity in diversity, not only of a mixed iconographic tradition, but more importantly of the very essence of catholicity. Christianity cannot be monopolised by any national group. It is not only Latin or Greek – or even Coptic – but universal. Athanasius, spanning East and West in defence of Jesus Christ, the one Redeemer of the world, is a striking witness to that fact.

Prayers before the Icon of St Athanasius

Lord Jesus Christ, eternal Son of the Father, true God
from true God, by the prayers of your servant
Athanasius: reveal to us the glory of your Godhead!
Lord Jesus Christ, eternal Son of the Father, light of light:
shine with the knowledge of your glory in the
darkness of our minds!
Lord Jesus Christ, eternal Son of the Father, risen to the
highest heavens: pour out on us the Holy Spirit, the
Lord and giver of life!

Almighty God, you raised up St Athanasius of Alexandria
to be an outstanding defender of the truth of Christ's
divinity. By his teaching and the protection of his prayers
may we advance daily in our knowledge and love of you,
through Christ our Lord. Amen.
(Prayer from the Roman Rite, adapted)

The Icon of St Dimitri of Rostov

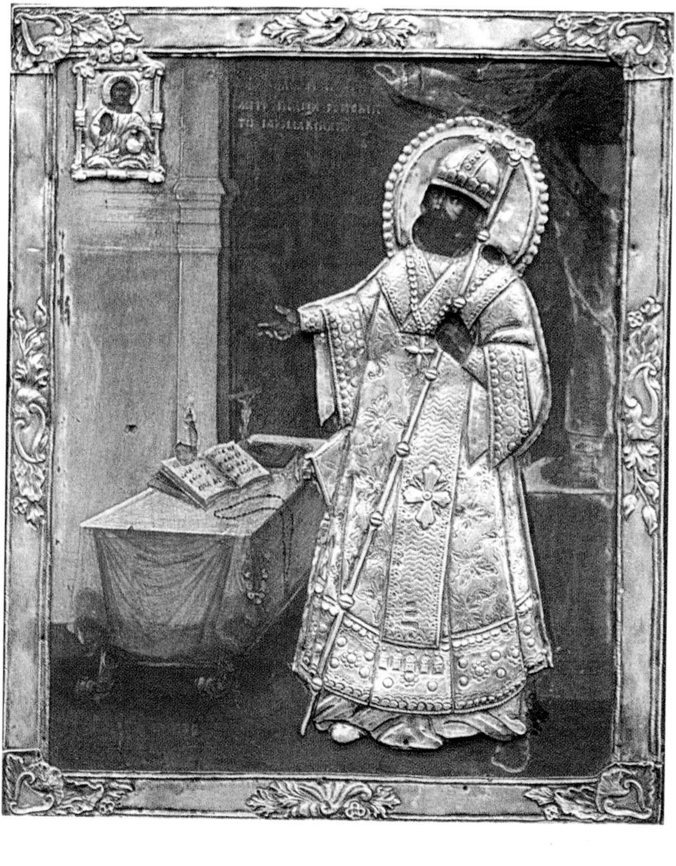

A Meditation on the Icon of
St Dimitri of Rostov

Remember your leaders, those who spoke the word of
God to you; consider the outcome of their way of life, and
imitate their faith.

(Hebrews 13:7)

From a strictly iconographic point of view, this icon is
rather less 'pure' than the others. Coming as it does from a
period in Russian history when contact with the authentic
Byzantine sources of Russian religious culture was somewhat weak, it mixes traditional Eastern motifs with influ-
ences derived from Western art.

Though basically Byzantine in inspiration, it leans
heavily in the direction of the Western artistic tradition. The
artist has used perspective, light and shade, in a thoroughly
Western way. This mingling of styles recalls the icon of St
Athanasius but the final product here is less well executed.
Unlike that image, this one is a little clumsy and heavy in
style. However, it does suggest the influence of popular
culture and is not devoid of a certain charm in this respect.

The saint is represented not against a transcendent gold
background, but within a very ordinary room furnished
with a small altar. He does not face out towards us, as in
the purest iconographical traditions. He turns slightly to
the side, although the chief intention of the artist is clearly
to direct our gaze to the small icon of Christ hanging on
the wall. There is a mundane, earthbound aspect to the
icon with its homely attention to everyday detail.

There are, however, obviously Orthodox elements to
tell us that it is an Eastern painting. The image of Christ on
the wall is a traditional icon of the *Pantokrator,* that is the

Lord Jesus as Ruler of the world. The saint himself is dressed in his *sakkos*, the Byzantine Episcopal vestment. He wears a Byzantine mitre, or *metra*, and carries the distinctive staff of an Orthodox bishop, called by the Greeks his *rabdos* and by the Russians his *posokh*. This is topped by two serpents which face one another, a sign of the prudence needed by a bishop.

The stylistic mixture, as with that of Athanasius, is particularly appropriate for the subject it depicts, since the Slavonic inscription indicates that we are looking at Saint Dimitri of Rostov (1651-1709) one of the greatest Russian bishops of the early modern period. Like the Russian church in general in this period, he was heavily influenced by Western theology and spirituality (translating the Latin prayer, *Anima Christi*, 'Soul of Christ', into Russian). Yet he remained deeply faithful to the Orthodox tradition in his spirituality, with a particular devotion to the Jesus prayer.

On the table lies a clear sign of his Orthodox faith, a woollen prayer-rope, the *komvoschoinion*, used by Orthodox Christians to help in saying the Jesus prayer. Through this powerful symbol of prayer, the icon shows one of the most important roles of the bishop: his call to be a man of prayer. Already in the earliest life of the church we see the apostles selecting others, traditionally identified as the first deacons, to carry out administrative work and social welfare, so as to leave themselves free for the ministry of the word and prayer (Acts 6:1-6).

Faced with the demands of leadership and administration, it can be easy for bishops to forget that prayer is meant to be their chief service to the church. Yet to be people of deep contemplative prayer and regular liturgical worship is how bishops can best lead their flocks and present them to God.

The icon of St Dimitri reminds us of this in several ways: The saint is dressed in his liturgical vestments, the clothing associated with leading public worship in the celebration of the divine liturgy (the eucharist) and in the daily hours of prayer (the divine office). It is the bishop's responsibility to proclaim the word of God to the people and in turn to speak the church's words of prayer to God. This is done in the name and person of Christ, in the strength of the Holy Spirit who anoints his ministers for this very purpose.

The bishop, high priest among the people, manifests and ministers the presence of the Lord. The prayer-rope on the table represents the call to pray unceasingly which has so impregnated the whole spiritual tradition of the Christian East. To pray incessantly, to maintain like the angelic hosts a perpetual watch before the face of God, to turn inward to the temple of the soul so as to experience God's indwelling presence: such is the goal of the spiritual life in the Christian East. The unbroken repetition of the holy name of Jesus, planting it deeply within the mind, creates a state of inner union with Christ, in which the memory of God grows unceasingly in the heart.

Finally, St Dimitri looks directly at the icon of Christ hanging upon the wall. Dimitri's doctrine and exemplary life were not the result of his own efforts. He drew his strength from the power of Christ whose love impelled him to the service of the church. Worship, perpetual prayer in the name of Jesus and constant gazing on the face of the incarnate Saviour, are the spiritual disciplines required to do the Lord's work in a fruitful way.

Commitment to these practices spiritually refines one's personality by conforming it to God's will. Then the grace to carry out one's mission in life, despite all difficulties, will be granted by God. Cut off from union with Christ, no Christian – still less one who has responsibility for others – can achieve anything good for anyone (John 15:5).

Appropriately, the icon of St Dimitri, like that of St Athanasius, is a cross-cultural image. Here it displays a mixture of the Latin and Russian traditions. Dimitri was a spiritual plant nourished by several streams, who yet remained firmly rooted in the soil of Russian Orthodoxy. He can serve as a reminder to Christians East and West, that the different churches are sisters in the one, universal family of churches.

Prayers before the Icon of St Dimitri

Lord Jesus Christ, Good Shepherd, by the prayers of St
    Dimitri, raise up faithful shepherds for your flock!
Lord Jesus Christ, Saviour of the world, by the prayers of
    St Dimitri, provide for your church in all its needs!
Lord Jesus Christ, gate of the sheepfold, by the prayers of
    St Dimitri, unite all Christians in love of your name!

Look to him and be radiant;
So your faces shall never be ashamed.
This poor man cried, and was heard by the Lord,
and was saved from every trouble. *(Psalm 34:5-6)*

Lord God, who gave the Holy Spirit of truth and love to your saint, Dimitri of Rostov: may we who honour him with our prayers learn from his example and be helped by his intercession. Grant this through Christ our Lord. Amen.
(Prayer from the Roman Rite, Office for Pastors, adapted)

A Meditation on the Icon of St Mary of Egypt

Truly the eye of the Lord is on those who fear him,
on those who hope in his steadfast love.
(Psalm 33:18)

This icon shows St Mary of Egypt, one of the early 'desert mothers'. Mary's remarkable life led to her intense veneration by Eastern Christians and even to an entire Sunday in Lent in the Byzantine Rite (the fifth) being devoted to her. Her biographer describes her as one who was almost frenetically sexually active, giving herself to many lovers. Even on board the boat she took to the Holy Land, she engaged in the same kind of activity. However, when Mary attempted to enter the Holy Sepulchre in Jerusalem on the feast of the Exaltation of the Cross, she felt herself prevented by an invisible force that would not allow her go through the door.

Pierced to the heart by compunction, she prayed before the icon of the Mother of God, only to find that on her second attempt she was actually impelled into the church by the same invisible force that had previously prevented her from entering. She went in, venerated the relic of the true cross and dedicated herself to conversion. After this, Mary retired to the desert where, living as a hermit, she devoted herself to a severe ascetic discipline of prayer and fasting.

Near the end of her life, after forty-seven years in the desert, she had a chance encounter with a monk named Zossima, who had gone to spend Lent in the wilderness in accordance with the custom of his monastic house. These monks traditionally stayed in the desert from the first Sunday of Lent until Palm Sunday. He recounted her life, in which he described her constant union with God. Zossima learnt that although unlettered, Mary knew holy scripture by heart, having been taught directly by the Word of God. On Holy Thursday he brought her communion. On returning the following year, he found her dead. Her biographer recounts that a lion helped Zossima to bury her body.

The two figures in this icon are striking examples of the way of asceticism in Eastern Christianity. On the left stands Zossima with hands outstretched to heaven in the early Christian gesture of prayer. He is very much the typical Orthodox monk, bearded, and clothed in the great monastic or angelic habit, the *Megaloschemos*. His scapular is emblazoned with the symbols of the passion in red embroidery as a sign that the monk walks consciously on the way of Christ's passion. The monastic descent into humility and self-abnegation is undertaken after the pattern of Christ, who became obedient even unto death on a cross (Philippians 2:8). Zossima represents the paradigm of 'institutional' monasticism.

Mary, for her part, is clad in the cloak given her by Zossima so as to cover her nakedness. Her body, emaciated by fasting and life in the desert, has been refined into the kind of flame-like form that speaks of ardent holiness to the Christians of the East. Her wild, unkempt appearance contrasts sharply with the 'institutional' monastic form of the monk, but the contrast is itself instructive. It reminds us that the monastic vocation comes from the Holy Spirit. God may call his servants into strange and even outlandish modes of behaviour which cannot be contained in institutional forms. Like the Byzantine and Russian 'holy fools', who followed extreme spiritual paths, even to the point of feigning madness, Mary's weird and wonderful life points to the unpredictability of God's Spirit, which blows wherever it wills (John 3:8).

At the top of the icon is a striking depiction of the face of Jesus, the kind traditionally known in the East as, *acheiropoetos*, or 'not made by human hands.' This iconographic type dates back to an early legend that Jesus once imprinted the likeness of his face on a handkerchief, which he sent to the King of Edessa. It is *the* icon of the holy face in the Christian East.

Mary's life embodies an idea that is sometimes present in works by Orthodox writers (such as Dostoyevsky). It is the difference between an 'official' monastic holiness, to some extent 'achieved' by an ascetical programme of co-operation with God, and therefore always in danger of degenerating into pride, and a more broken, and therefore purer kind of holiness, whereby God reaches down to someone in the depths of degradation, and transforms her by his grace.

Mary of Egypt is a potent reminder to all who follow official programmes aimed at holiness that salvation is always God's free gift. Infirmity, weakness and even sin are the raw material of humility, which remind us of the constant need for grace (2 Corinthians 12:6-10).

Her behaviour might be interpreted today as a compulsive sexual disorder, a psychological problem stemming from self-loathing and a frantic need to be loved. In the end, by God's grace, she found such love not in many human 'lovers' but in the one divine lover – the God of beauty, goodness and grace. Therefore she has become a shining witness to the love of God, which reaches down to save us in our poverty. The fruit of such love is the purest kind of humility, deeper than any ascetical path we might choose to follow. In this icon Mary does not pray, for Orthodox tradition recognises that there is a state even beyond prayer in which the heart is rapt forever in love on the face of the Lord. Mary does not pray. She has become a channel of grace – and so she blesses.

Prayers before the Icon of St Mary of Egypt

Hurrying to see the cross, O Mary, you were enlightened by its light through the providence of your crucified Lord. You yourself were crucified to the world, O saint most worthy of our praise. Although you once led many into evil through your lust, you now shine like the sun in your holiness, and have become for sinners a heavenly guide.
(Byzantine hymn to Mary of Egypt, adapted)

Lord Jesus Christ, by the prayers of our holy mother,
    Mary of Egypt, and St Zossima your servant, pardon
    all our sins and offences, for you are alone are the
    lover of humankind!
Lord Jesus Christ, you restore lost innocence by your
    resurrection from the dead: grant us innocence of
    heart and a spirit of simplicity!
Lord Jesus Christ, you are the origin of our deepest
    desire. Satisfy our hunger for love with the fire of
    your Holy Spirit!

God, thou great symmetry,
who put a biting lust in me
from whence my sorrows spring.
For all the frittered days
that I have spent in shapeless ways.
give me one perfect thing.
(From a poem by A. Wickham.)

Hear, O Lord, and be gracious to me!
O Lord, be my helper!

You have turned my mourning into dancing;
you have taken off my sackcloth
and clothed me with joy,
so that my soul may praise you and not be silent.
O Lord my God, I will give thanks to you forever.
(Psalm 30:10-12)

Two Icons of the Deesis

I urge that supplications, prayers, intercessions and thanks-
givings be made for everyone.
(1 Timothy 2: 1)

These two icons represent the mystery of supplication, of
prayer and intercession focused on the glory of Christ as it
is revealed within the community of the church.

A Meditation on the Great Deesis

'… they fell on their faces before the throne and
worshipped God, singing, 'Amen! Blessing and glory and
wisdom and thanksgiving and honour and power and
might be to our God forever and ever! Amen.'
(Revelation 7:12)

The iconographic type known as the *Deesis*, a Greek word
meaning supplication, is a complex arrangement illustrat-
ing the mystery of prayer to Christ the Lord. It depicts the
praying Mother of God and St John the Baptist flanking the
Lord Jesus, who is enthroned in the centre. Behind him at
the back of the image are archangels, apostles and church
fathers. Kneeling at the left hand of Christ is an early saint,
Paraskeve. History has recorded almost nothing about her,
but she has been retained in the liturgical memory of the
churches of the East as a martyr for Christ.

In the foreground of the icon two monastic saints make
a dramatic gesture of humility and supplication, the great
metanoia, or full prostration of the body. To perform this

action in the Byzantine tradition, the sign of the cross is made and then the body is thrown forward on to the ground to express humility, spiritual indigence and adoration, or *proskynesis*. The gestures occur very frequently in Orthodox worship, but never more dramatically than in the prayer of St Ephrem recited during the Offices of Great Lent. Eastern Christianity accords a prominent place to the role of the body in the spiritual life, teaching that it must be refined by fasting, anointed with oil and honoured with incense. It is always associated with the deepest kind of prayer.

For the Eastern Christian there can be no false dichotomy between the inner and outer dimensions of the person, between the soul and the flesh. The human being is one before God with a mysterious union of soul and body. The soul is the interior of the body, the body the manifestation of the soul. These find their point of contact in the heart. This unity is the space in which God manifests his presence. The Christian prays therefore as a whole person. The depths of the soul must rise up into the crucible of the heart, there to meet the grace of the Holy Spirit, whose energies penetrate it, entering the body through the oil of anointing.

The 'athletic' aspects of prayer, that is the use of physical methods in Eastern Christianity, remind us that human beings are not ghostly souls temporarily inhabiting bodies, but persons of sense and spirit, in whose hearts the Holy Spirit dwells as in a temple.

The saints in this icon represent many categories of holiness in the Christian church. There are angels, the bearers of God's enlightening wisdom to humankind. They keep a perpetual watch before the throne of God, ever ready to do his will in conveying heavenly messages to his witnesses on earth (Psalm 103:20-21). There are apostles, the pillars and foundations of the church (Galatians 2:9; Ephesians 2:20), who, in the words of the Roman liturgy, 'from their place in heaven, guide us still'. There are also theologians and fathers of the church whose task it is to communicate divine wisdom through preaching and teaching after they have tasted it in prayer. Then there are martyrs who lay down their lives for the truth, and monks who represent the dedicated holiness to which all the baptised are called.

This large gathering accompanying the *Theotokos* and John the Baptist as they pray before the Lord, represents the unity of the praying church as she converges on her bridegroom and head. He is Christ the Lord, God's incarnate Wisdom and eternal Son, Lord of the Universe and of time itself, Alpha and Omega (John 1:14-17; Revelation 1:8). In him divinity is forever united to humanity: in him are hidden all the treasures of wisdom and knowledge (Colossians 2:2-3).

Prayer to Christ means opening one's mind and heart to the wisdom streaming from him so as to be enlightened and instructed in the things of God. One must look towards him for the radiance of his light (Psalm 34:5), for it is in contemplating Jesus the incarnate Wisdom that true knowledge of God is learnt. Hence one of the greatest Eastern monastic teachers of prayer, Evagrius (d. 399) once wrote: 'If you pray truly you are a theologian for a theologian is one who prays.' Both Eastern and Western teachers agree that in reaching the summits of divine knowledge abandonment of oneself is essential. The human intellect must stretch itself to the limit in plumbing the depths of revelation, but the purest knowledge of God is learnt only in the darkness of faith, in suffering, and in love. Both St Dionysios and St Thomas Aquinas describe this as a 'suffering' of divine things, a passion of the intellect in the face of God's unfathomable infinity. In learning this kind of prayer – the summit of theology – the active voice of effort must be transformed into the passive voice of surrender to the mystery.

This icon of the great *Deesis*, like the fuller form of the Jesus prayer, is *the* icon of the church as a praying communion. The whole church assembles around the Lord, to worship him and pray to him for mercy and for light. It is the icon of the whole church, Mount Zion the city of the living God, the heavenly Jerusalem, united in adoration before the throne of God and before the Lamb (Hebrews 12:18-24; Revelation 7:9-17). The church on earth unites with this church of heaven in prayer, as she journeys onward guided only by the light of faith.

Prayers before the Icon of the Great *Deesis*

All you angels and archangels,
thrones, dominations, principalities and powers,
hosts of heaven,
cherubim and seraphim,
patriarchs and prophets,
holy teachers of the law of God,
apostles and all Christ's martyrs,
holy confessors,
virgins of the Lord and anchorites,
and all God's holy ones: intercede for us!
(Adapted from the Benedictine Office of Vespers for All Saints)

May Mary the holy one, and all the saints, intercede for us with the Lord that we may be helped and saved by Christ, who lives and reigns forever and ever.
(Prayer from the Monastic Office.)

O Lord and Master of my life, give me not a spirit of laziness, curiosity, lust for power and idle talking!
But give to me your servant a spirit of sobriety, humility, patience, and love!
O my Lord and King, grant that I may see my own faults and not condemn those of my brothers and sisters, for you are blessed to the ages of ages! Amen.
(Prayer of St Ephrem, Byzantine Office of Lent)

Lord Jesus Christ, Son and Word of the living God, by the prayers of your most pure Mother, of the holy Baptist and forerunner John, of the angels, patriarchs and prophets and of the martyrs and saints, send down on us the promised Holy Spirit that we may praise and glorify you, now and forever!
Lord Jesus Christ, Son and Word of the living God, by the prayers of your most pure Mother and of all your saints, guide your church on the path that leads to life!
Lord Jesus Christ, Son and Word of the living God, by the prayers of your most pure Mother and of all your saints, bring all creation to worship at the throne of the most holy Trinity!

A Meditation on the Small Deesis

Look, here is the Lamb of God. (John 1:36)

Just as there is a shorter form of the Jesus prayer encapsulating the essence of the larger form, so there is also a smaller, more concentrated form of the *deesis* icon.

In the examples shown here (three little icons constituting a portable, folding triptych) the core of the *deesis* arrangement is represented by the figure of Christ, this time flanked only by his Mother and Saint John the Baptist. The icons, which are of great purity, have been written with considerable skill. They are highlighted by the turquoise stones surrounding them. This portable triptych can remind us that icons are never static objects but bearers of a presence. They are moveable things accompanying believers on their journey towards the kingdom of heaven.

In the Orthodox world many legendary stories exist of icons travelling from place to place. Symbolically, this represents the dynamic nature of the icon as a place of movement and interaction between the divine and human worlds. It also recalls the constant practice in Orthodox countries of processing with the icons in towns and villages and through the countryside. They are never merely static objects.

The smaller form of the *deesis,* like the larger type, emphasises prayer, the supplication and intercession offered for the church on earth to Christ the Lord, by the two greatest saints in heaven. But there is also a deeper theological meaning in the arrangement. As is so often the case in Eastern iconography, the images convey important Christian doctrines. The two figures flanking Jesus can tell us much about the mystery of Christ.

John the Baptist has always received considerable veneration among the Christians of the East. They refer to him as the *Prodromos*, or Forerunner, who went ahead of the Lord to prepare his way. He was sent, as the angel Gabriel prophesied at his conception, to make ready a people who would be fit to receive the Messiah (Luke 1:13-19). John is frequently depicted in iconography, appearing in the scene of Christ's baptism and again in that of his own martyrdom. He was decapitated at the wish of the scheming Herodias and her treacherous daughter, because of the moral turpitude of Herod, the weak, adulterous Ruler (Mark 6:17-29; Matthew 14:1-12).

But John is also, like the fiery prophet Elijah, venerated in the Christian East as a proto-monk. His ascetical existence in the desert prefigured the path so many Christian ascetics would later take into the wilderness, to do battle with Satan and live in direct dependence on the grace of God (Matthew 3:1-12). John was indeed, as Jesus said, a great prophet, a new Elijah heralding the coming of the Christ (Matthew 11:7-16). He was a witness who testified to the true light that enlightens everyone who comes into the world (John 1:6-9). In the words of Jesus, he was, 'a burning and shining lamp' (John 5:35). St Augustine observed that John was the voice making known the coming of the Word. But he was also given another extraordinary accolade by Jesus, who showered on him the highest praise:

> *Truly I tell you, among those born of women no one has arisen greater than John the Baptist,*

and then went on to add,

> *Yet the least in the kingdom of heaven is greater than he.*

(Matthew 11:11)

This is where the mystery of Mary, the *Theotokos,* enters in. In the gospel of St Luke she is depicted as one of the poor in spirit, wholly dedicated to the will of God (Luke 1:26-38). Mary, as the chosen daughter of Zion, opens her heart in faith to God's command, as a consequence of which she bears his incarnate Son. She is set before us as the contemplative disciple, pondering God's word in her heart (Luke 2: 51), putting herself completely at his disposal. Even though Eastern Christianity does not speak as Roman Catholicism does of Mary's immaculate conception, it does honour her as the most perfect disciple and the first of the redeemed, sinless through the grace of her son.

In this icon we see some of these great themes depicted. On the one side we have the summit of the holiness possible under the Old Covenant, as John, the last of the prophets, bears witness to the incarnate Word. In pointing to Christ, John the friend of the bridegroom, defers to the bridegroom of the church who increases even as John decreases (John 3:29).

On the other side we see Mary, first in the kingdom of heaven, first to receive the overshadowing of the Holy Spirit (Luke 1:35) in the new dispensation. Both bear witness to Christ. John does so as the conclusion of the prophetic tradition of Israel. Mary gives her witness as the first fruits of the new covenant. She exults in God her Saviour (Luke 1:47). Both draw their life and mission from the person of incarnate Wisdom, the Son of God whom they each serve in their own appointed way. From their place in heaven they help the church by prayer, to follow in his way. This is their role as intercessors. They direct our gaze to Christ, the hope of all the nations, the one in whom the fullness of grace and truth inheres (John 1:17).

Christ is the Lamb of God who takes away the sins of the world (John 1:36), a Lamb led to the slaughter, silently slain for the sins of others (Isaiah 53:7), a Lamb destined by God since before the foundation of the world, and revealed at the end of the ages for our salvation (1 Peter 1:19-20). To him be glory forever!

Prayers before the Icon of the Small *Deesis*

Lord Jesus my light, by the prayers of Mary your Mother
and of St John the Baptist, enlighten my heart!
Lord Jesus my light, by the prayers of Mary your Mother
and of St John the Baptist, open my ears to your word!
Lord Jesus my light, by the prayers of Mary your Mother
and of St John the Baptist, enlighten all people who
come into this world!

O blessed saint filled with heavenly merits,
O dweller in the wilderness,
O mightiest of martyrs, and greatest among the prophets:
make straight our crooked ways and break our hearts of stone.
(Hymn for the feast of St John the Baptist, Roman Rite, adapted.)

Worthy is the Lamb that was slaughtered
to receive power and wealth and wisdom and might
and honour and glory and blessing!
To the one seated on the throne and to the Lamb,
be blessing and honour and glory and might
forever and ever!
(Revelation 5:12-13)

Behold the Lamb of God! Behold the one who takes away the sins of the world! Blessed are all those who are called to share in the wedding banquet of the lamb!
(Prayer before communion in the Mass of the Roman Rite, based on words from St John the Baptist)

Two Icons of the Holy Trinity:
the Eastern and the Western Trinity

*The grace of the Lord Jesus Christ, the love of God, and
the communion of the Holy Spirit be with all of you.*
(2 Corinthians 13:13)

Since we began our meditations with the icon of Christ, it
is fitting to conclude with two images of the Holy Trinity,
for the Trinity has been revealed to us through the coming
of Christ and the descent of the Holy Spirit. In approaching God, we should not begin with abstract philosophical
notions of the deity, but allow God's incarnate Word to
speak to us of who he really is. Jesus Christ, who is closest
to the Father's heart, is the one who makes him known
(John 1:18), for no one knows the Son except the Father, or
the Father except the Son – and those to whom the Son
chooses to reveal him (Matthew 11:25-27). He reveals God
to us as a communion of Persons, Father, Son and Holy
Spirit (John 14:15-17), as the Byzantine liturgy puts it, 'one
in substance and undivided'.

The Trinity is not a kind of word game, or a series of
mathematical problems one might solve by reasoning. It is
the fullness of divine revelation – the truth that makes us
free (John 8:31-32), an abundant life that flows to us from
above (John 10:10). It is the revelation of a transcendent
mystery, high above all human knowledge. Were it not for
the appearance of the eternal *Logos* in flesh and blood as
the Saviour Jesus Christ, and the outpouring of the
Pneuma, or divine Spirit through him, we would not have
any access to the hidden, inner life of God. Indeed even
after they have come and brought us knowledge, God

remains eternally a mystery, a bottomless sea of divinity into whose immensity we may dive, but whose limitless depths we shall never fully fathom. He dwells in unapproachable light beyond all vision (1 Timothy 6:16).

But in fact Jesus Christ *has* come in the power of the Holy Spirit, and has brought us the revelation of the truth (1 John 5:20), the knowledge that God is love (1 John 4:16). Thanks to the light that has been given us, we can, however haltingly, form ideas and images about the inner life of God. *Theologia*, or theology, in the understanding of the Eastern churches, is specifically this knowledge of the Trinity. But such knowledge is strictly possible only on the basis of the *oikonomia*, the plan or dispensation, the saving acts – especially his death and resurrection – which Jesus carried out for our redemption.

As Vladimir Lossky once observed, the theological knowledge of the Trinity entails a kind of crucifixion for the mind. In approaching it, another kind of understanding must be used, for the mystery demands humility of mind and heart if we are to speak about it adequately. There can be no attempt to pull away the veils from the inscrutable divine essence, or to peer into what has not been revealed. We need to approach this mystery in prayer, staying close to what the Lord himself has told us: for the mystery is God himself, who gives his grace to the humble. The rays of light flowing from the Trinity are numberless, but three may be considered.

Firstly, there is a *taxis*, or order in the Persons of the Godhead. The Father is the primal Font, or Source of all divinity. In this sense, but *only* in this sense, he is prior to the other two Persons, since he is the Principle from whom they come into being (John 14:28). This is an eternal process, since he begets his Word and sends forth his Spirit, consubstantial with himself, in a perpetual stillness beyond time.

Unfortunately, in the course of history a major difference of understanding has arisen here between the Orthodox East and the Catholic West. For the East, closely following the order described by Jesus, the Spirit comes forth eternally from the Father and rests upon the Son, but is not actively produced by the Son himself. The *incarnate* Son, after his death and resurrection receives the Spirit, whom he and the Father send upon the church (John 15:26). Orthodoxy acknowledges that the Spirit comes from the Son in the economy of salvation, but denies that he is productive of the Spirit in the inner life of God. Beyond this it will not go, since it keeps strictly to the revealed data.

In addition, Orthodoxy generally begins with the revelation of the Persons before considering their unity of essence. This order is reflected in what the Creed of Nicaea-Constantinople (381), once common to East and West, says about the Spirit: '(I believe) in the Holy Spirit, the Lord and giver of life, who proceeds from the *Father*.' By contrast, Western theologians tend to begin with the unity of God's nature, and then go on to look at the relations arising within it. The two approaches should in fact be complementary.

However, in some local churches in the West (though not originally at Rome), to defend the full divinity of Christ, and his equality with the Father, theologians following the lead of St Augustine inserted the word *filioque*, meaning 'and the Son', into the clause in the Creed about who produces the Spirit. Despite the fact that St Maximos the Confessor, one of the greatest fathers of the undivided

Catholic-Orthodox church, was prepared to allow this usage to stand, it was destined to become a bitter bone of contention. Eventually accepted by Rome, it became inextricably mixed with ecclesiastical politics and is still a source of controversy and division.

Some Orthodox see this as the source of all evil, suggesting that the Western churches forget the Holy Spirit, subordinating him to the Son, or worse to the earthly church. This claim is not without some basis in the history of the church. However, great Eastern saints of the first millennium managed to keep communion even when the *filioque* was being used. An ecumenical spirit now tries to find the deeper truth behind such terms so as not to break communion – the most important aspect of the Christian life.

It is legitimate, however, for Catholics to hope and pray that one day the *filioque*, the source of so much tension, might be removed from the Creed, so that we can profess it together again in the original text composed when Latins and Greeks were one. However, despite these disputes, we should not forget what the order in the Trinity really means. The Father, Source and Goal of all things, sends his Spirit to us through the risen Son, while we for our part return to him in prayer through Christ, in the power of the Spirit. Perhaps if theologians spent less energy arguing about where precisely the Spirit *comes from,* and gave more attention to what he does when he *arrives* among us, the whole church might benefit more.

The second ray of light pertains to God as a communion of Persons, joined in an eternal relationship of love. The Father begets the Word and breathes out the Spirit, but the Spirit *rests* eternally on the Son before he comes to us, through him, in time. In the Western understanding (derived from St Augustine), the Spirit is the fruit of their mutual love. Similarly St Gregory Palamas was prepared to call him the 'joy' of the Father and the Son. Fr Dumitru Staniloae, a married Orthodox priest, once suggested that the third Person, rather like a child in a human family, by emerging within the all-absorbing love of the other two, represents God's capacity to open outwards to others.

As the Western mystic Meister Eckhart liked to say, this bubbling cauldron of love boils over, pouring out of itself and allowing the possibility of creation. God is supremely free. The Trinity does not *have* to create. But when God chooses to do so, he is able to because his very own existence in the three divine Persons is a 'letting-be', a blessing of otherness in the unity of love. Creation, as St Augustine intuited, is stamped with the sign of the Trinity, and once the mystery has been revealed, one can detect its traces everywhere.

The third ray of light pertains to created love. Human beings, made in God's image, are meant to mirror the likeness of the eternal Trinity. Just as Father, Son and Holy Spirit keep nothing for themselves but exist in mutual self-donation, so human beings are called to live a life of relationship, a life of mutual self-giving, modelled on the Trinity. To call us back to this sublime vision of existence, when we fell into the fragmentation and disharmony of sin, the eternal Son consented to become like us, to restore in us the likeness of the Triune God. He showed us most especially by his passion that love is our vocation, that love configures us to God. In this divine work all three Persons were involved, for the Father surrendered his Son into the hands of sinners (Romans 5:8), the Son offered himself on the cross for us (Ephesians 5:2), and the sacrifice was consummated in the power of the Holy Spirit (Hebrews 9:14). The supreme sign of the Trinity is therefore the sign of the cross.

The church, born at the foot of the cross, is called to be the community of those who stand under it, who model their lives on it. Such a vision of the Trinity, revealed in crucified love, has profound implications for every aspect of Christian life – for ecclesiology, ethics, liturgy, ministry and mission. In the words of St Cyprian, quoted in the documents of the Second Vatican Council, the church is a people brought into unity from the unity of the Father, the Son and the Holy Spirit. But above all, it transforms our understanding of God. He is not some distant cosmic potentate, but the revelation of redeeming, sharing love in the holy and undivided Trinity.

The Eastern Trinity

A Meditation on the Eastern Trinity

Let mutual love continue. Do not neglect to show
hospitality to strangers, for by doing that
some have entertained angels without knowing it.
(Hebrews 13:1-2)

This type of icon is very ancient. Its symbolic form is the one the Eastern churches consider the most appropriate for depicting the Trinity. The icon is based on the story of how Abraham and Sarah entertained three strangers at the oak of Mamre, and on account of this is known in Greek as the icon of the *philoxenia*, or hospitality (Genesis 18:1-15). Tradition soon identified the men with angels, seeing in them a *theophany,* or manifestation of the Trinity. In Russia the great Trinity icon painted by St Andrei Rublev, was regarded by a church council (1551) as the most perfect of icons and an example to be followed. The Russian icon shown here is part of a panel depicting the great feasts of the liturgical year. It stands within the tradition of Rublev's work.

The scene is reduced to the barest minimum – the three main figures, the tree, the house and the table with its vessel. This is no longer an earthly meal but a heavenly symposium. The three angels, actually the three divine Persons, are engaged in the discussion during which the redemption of the world is being planned. Protestant theology calls this the *pactum salutis*, or eternal covenant of redemption, made between the Father and the Son, which in the Holy Spirit will be translated into flesh and blood in the incarnation and death of Christ. The Son speaks the words from Psalm 40 (7-8), which the author of the letter to the Hebrews (10:7) puts into his mouth as he takes up his mission to the world: 'Here

I am; in the scroll of the book it is written of me. I delight to do your will, O my God!'

As the Russian theologian Sergius Bulgakov taught, the cross manifests the eternal sacrifice of love, offered and received, within the very heart of the Trinity. This icon testifies that the love revealed in time has an eternal foundation. Theology, the inner life of the Trinity, grounds the plan of salvation in the work of Christ. Opinions differ as to which of the divine Persons is symbolised by the angels but I tend to see the Father as the central angel. This corresponds more closely to the triangular symbolism in the Eastern construction of the Trinity, whereby he, as Source, begets the Son and emits the Spirit. Yet the three figures together are contained within a circle, to represent the reciprocity of love.

They sit around a table at the banquet of the kingdom, the heavenly source and fulfilment of the earthly eucharist. A space left open at the front shows that the Trinity is open to participation through the mystery of the eucharistic meal. This is the icon of the beginning and the end. The beginning, since it shows the original divine decree, made from all eternity to invite humanity into the life of God. The end, because it shows that the table is set and the banquet of eternal life prepared. Blessed indeed are those who are called – and who come with eager joy – to sit at such a table in such a kingdom!

A Meditation on the Western Trinity
'Abba! Father!'
(Romans 8:15)

This icon shows a later way of depicting the Trinity. Like much else in the nineteenth century Russian church, it shows a strong influence from Western ideas. It therefore represents in some sense a declension from the strictest Eastern tradition. Here, the symbolic purity of the angelic forms in the previous depiction, and the subtlety of their triangular-circular evocation of the *perichoresis*, or solemn dance of love between the three Persons, has been sacrificed to an anthropomorphic depiction showing the Father as an old man, the Son in the incarnate form proper to him, and the Holy Spirit as a dove. The latter depictions are possible, since the Word became flesh and the Spirit was manifested at Christ's baptism in the likeness of a dove (Luke 3:22).

It is, however, strictly speaking, impossible to show the Father in any form, except symbolically. He is the invisible God (Colossians 1:15). Since he did not become incarnate, he cannot be seen by any human eye. The Russian church has at times therefore attempted to proscribe this type of icon, but the human need to visualise God has repeatedly led to the Father being depicted in human form. In fact there is a biblical model operating in this kind of icon. It is that of the mysterious white haired, white clad, 'Ancient of Days', seated on a throne of fire. He is described by Daniel who saw him in a dream concerning the last judgement (Daniel 7).

A human figure appeared before this Ancient One and received from him an undying dominion over all peoples, nations and languages. It was natural that Christians should see in these figures the promised Christ, entering into his glory in the presence of the eternal Father. The same kind of imagery is present also in the book of the Revelation (4). Hence, although this Western kind of Trinity icon is less pure than the other type, it is nevertheless based on scriptural references rich in religious associations. The fact that it shares a space on the same festal icon, shows that it too has a role to play in communicating the knowledge of the mystery.

But there is a deeper truth than this concealed within the icon, a truth derived from the Western theology by which it has been influenced. In the writings of the Latin fathers (especially St Augustine) and the medieval mystics (especially St Bernard, the Dominicans Eckhart and Tauler, and blessed John Ruusbroec) a special emphasis was placed on our participation in the common life of the three divine Persons. The Holy Spirit, the love of the Father and the Son, is poured out in our hearts, to lift us up and insert us into the relationship of love between the Father and the Son.

We are made children of God, adopted through the grace of the incarnate Son. We are begotten with the Son, into whose mode of being grace inserts us. We receive through him a share in his capacity to transmit the Holy Spirit, the power he shares with the Father. For the Western church, the Spirit is the 'kiss of love' between the Father and the Son: we share in this eternal kiss between the heavenly Persons, in an unending embrace of love. There is nothing here that contradicts the ethos of the Christian East. A somewhat different understanding of the mystery is evident, but it comes to us from the mystics of the Western church.

This icon, imperfect as it is, reminds us of our destiny: to enter on the wings of the dove into the common life of the Trinity and be taken up forever into their eternal embrace. Then we will be one with God in the experience that the Latin mystics call *fruitio,* an overwhelming experience of joy. With the Eastern church we know that this is nothing less than the vision of the Father through the Son in the Holy Spirit's light. It is the transfigured life of everlasting love. May the All-Holy Trinity bring us to this life! Amen!

Prayers before the Icons of the Trinity

Glory be to the Father, and to the Son and to the Holy Spirit. To the one true God be glory: and on us, mercy and compassion forever more.
(Prayer from the Syrian liturgy.)

The Father is my hope!
The Son is my refuge!
The Holy Spirit is my protection!
All-Holy Trinity, glory to you!
(Prayer from the Byzantine Rite)

O Holy God!
O Holy and strong One!
O Holy and immortal One!
Have mercy on us.
(The Trisagion, used in many Eastern liturgies)

Through Christ,
with Christ,
and in Christ,
in the unity of the Holy Spirit,
all glory and honour is yours, Almighty Father,
forever and ever. Amen!
(Doxology from the Mass of the Roman Rite)

Lord Jesus Christ, light of the Father's face, show us your
    mercy!
Lord Jesus Christ, wisdom of God, fill us with your glory!
Lord Jesus Christ, bearer of the Holy Spirit, breathe forth
    your love into our hearts!

Daring to glorify your eternal Father, and you and your
Holy Spirit, O Christ our God, we cry out like the
Cherubim, Holy, Holy, Holy are you our God! By the
prayers of the Mother of God, have mercy on us!
(Hymn from the Byzantine Rite)

Appendix
The art of making icons

The first icons (examples of which can be seen in St Catherine's monastery at Mt Sinai) resemble in appearance and technique the famous funerary portraits found at Fayum in Egypt. They were made in the technique known as wax encaustic, in which the colours were probably mixed into hot wax and applied to boards with a spatula. It is important to note, however, that Christian icons are not simply portraits of the dead, but images of the incarnate God and the saints who live with him in glory. After the defeat of iconoclasm the use of egg tempera developed. Iconographers eschew the use of oil as a medium.

In egg tempera, the colours are mixed with egg yolk and water. This quick-drying mixture gives a smooth, shining finish. The paint is applied to a board (sometimes covered with strips of linen), which has been treated to prevent cracking, warping and splitting (by fixing slats to its back). It is also covered with a layer of gesso (a mixture of chalk and size), which is burnished before painting begins. Gold leaf is applied over another substance called bole (made from red or yellow earth). The final stage is the application of glazes.

In Russia in particular, the great subtlety and translucency of colour achieved by the icon painters produced the effect of a refined spiritual sensibility and of the transfiguration of matter by light. Unfortunately many icons are veiled by a metal cover, known in the Russian tradition as an *oklad*. This conceals the beauty behind it, but highlights the sacred, mysterious nature of the image.